Praise for *The Buddhist and the Ethicist*

"A wonderful book that does what philosophy and religious teachings are supposed to do: challenge us to think better, to live better, and to be better."
—RYAN HOLIDAY, podcast host and author of *The Daily Stoic*

"A remarkable and historical meeting of minds between one of the greatest philosophers of our times and a leading proponent of Buddhist ethics, both of whom aim at doing as much good as possible to all sentient beings without discrimination."
—MATTHIEU RICARD, author of *Altruism* and *A Plea for Animals*

"This probing exploration illuminates key concepts in the Buddhist and utilitarian traditions and reveals an underlying unity; these two schools of thought, though quite different in cultural ancestry, exhibit much commonality of purpose and spirit as they address some of life's most important and challenging questions."
—ROBERT WRIGHT, author of *Why Buddhism Is True*

"A fascinating exchange between two brilliant and wide-ranging thinkers. I guarantee you will rethink views you have on different ethical questions. I know I'll be returning to this valuable collection time and time again."
—MARC BEKOFF, coauthor of *The Animals' Agenda*

"A timely and stimulating dialogue that examines relevant social issues and transcends cultures and countries."
—SULAK SIVARAKSA, author, activist, and cofounder of the International Network of Engaged Buddhists

"Singer and Chao-Hwei show us how to have constructive, respectful dialogue about values—a skill more vitally important now than ever before. They remind us that it is possible to begin from seemingly conflicting points of view and, through open-minded conversation, to find and expand common ground."

—JESSICA PIERCE, author of *Who's a Good Dog? And How to Be a Better Human*

"A must-read for those seeking to expand their understanding of social justice, altruism, and pressing issues of our time, through Buddhist and Western ethical thought."

—NETIWIT CHOTIPHATPHAISAL, student activist, author, and engaged Buddhist

The Buddhist
and the Ethicist

Conversations on Effective
Altruism, Engaged Buddhism,
and How to Build a Better World

PETER SINGER AND SHIH CHAO-HWEI

 SHAMBHALA

Shambhala Publications, Inc.
2129 13th Street
Boulder, Colorado 80302
www.shambhala.com

Cover art: THEPALMER/iStock and clu/iStock
Cover design: Erin Seaward-Hiatt

9 8 7 6 5 4 3 2 1

First Edition
Printed in the United States of America

Shambhala Publications makes every effort
to print on acid-free, recycled paper.
Shambhala Publications is distributed worldwide by
Penguin Random House, Inc., and its subsidiaries.

Library of Congress Cataloging-in-Publication Data
Names: Singer, Peter, 1946– author. | Zhaohui, Shi, 1957– author.
Title: The Buddhist and the ethicist: conversations on effective altruism,
    engaged Buddhism, and how to build a better world / Peter Singer and
    Shih Chao-Hwei.
Description: Boulder: Shambhala, 2023. | Includes index.
Identifiers: LCCN 2023010760 | ISBN 9781645472179 (trade paperback)
Subjects: LCSH: Buddhist ethics.
Classification: LCC BJ1289 .S545 2023 | DDC 294.3/5—dc23/eng/20230407
LC record available at https://lccn.loc.gov/2023010760

Contents

Preface

Differences and Convergences

I am not, and never have been, a religious person. I have spent my life teaching and researching philosophy, particularly ethics, and I base my beliefs on evidence and reasoning, not faith. That puts me at odds with the systems of belief that are sometimes described as "the world's major religions," a category that typically includes Buddhism. Yet since I was a student at university, I have found Buddhism to be closer to my way of thinking than other major religions. Buddhists do not believe in a god or a divine creator. So should we really think of Buddhism as a religion, or is it rather a philosophy of life, in the broad sense of an understanding of human psychology and an approach to how best to live?

When I was still a graduate student in philosophy, I came to see that there is no justification for our exclusion of animals from the circle of beings to whom we have ethical obligations, and I stopped eating meat. Some people asked me if this view had anything to do with Buddhism. It didn't, but it did give me a sense of affinity between my own ideas and Buddhism, because the Buddhist precept of refraining from taking life includes all sentient beings. This is, in my view, a distinct improvement over the Christian, Jewish, and Islamic religious traditions, which limit their injunctions against killing solely to members of our own species.

Nevertheless, there seemed to be some aspects of Buddhism that I could not accept. Do Buddhists really believe that if we act wrongly, we will inevitably suffer for it, as the popular understanding of the doctrine of karma suggests? That would be a complete answer to the question "Why should I act ethically?" with which philosophers since Plato have grappled, without finding, in my view, a convincing answer. But it is easy to think of people who have done great harm to others and yet were able to live long and happy lives. Some Buddhists would say that those who have caused harm will be reincarnated and their next life will be miserable, but that seems no more plausible than the Christian idea that they will burn in hell for all eternity.

I also had some ethical problems with Buddhism. For one thing, when visiting countries like Thailand and Japan, where there are many Buddhists, I found very few vegetarians. I was surprised to find that even among Buddhist monastics, many eat meat or fish, despite the fact that this obviously makes them complicit in the killing of animals. Of course, Buddhists would not be the only people to fail to live up to the precepts of their religion. Jesus is quoted in the Gospels as saying that it is easier for a camel to go through the eye of a needle than for a rich man to enter the kingdom of God, but there are plenty of rich Christians. Still, the acceptance of meat-eating by Buddhists, and the apparent absence of efforts by Buddhist leaders to do anything about it, was disappointing.

There is also a broader difference between my utilitarian view and what I took to be the Buddhist view of how we ought to live. Utilitarianism is concerned about the consequences of what we do or do not do. Utilitarians hold that we ought to do as much good as we can for all sentient beings, so utilitarianism encourages activism. Buddhism, as I understood it, encourages contemplation, focusing on meditation to improve oneself, rather than on acting to make the world a better place. I could not endorse that set of priorities.

———

In 2014, Venerable Shih Chao-Hwei, whom I had met many years earlier at a conference, invited me to speak at a conference in Taiwan titled "Animal Liberation, Animal Rights, and Equal Ecological Rights: Dialogues between Eastern and Western Philosophies and Religions." She also organized a tour for me and other conference guests to Hualien City to meet Master Cheng Yen, a Buddhist female monastic who in 1996 founded the Tzu Chi Foundation, a Buddhist humanitarian organization. What we saw was most impressive, but for me the journey itself was even more significant, because in several conversations with Chao-Hwei, I learned that her understanding of Buddhism had led her to be not only a vegetarian but also an activist in many of the areas that concerned me—including, of course, the ethical treatment of animals, as well as aid to people in great need and the empowerment of those who are marginalized, especially women.

On the train to Hualien City and over delicious vegetarian meals during our travels, Chao-Hwei explained the bodhisattva tradition in Buddhism. Bodhisattvas are enlightened people who choose not to achieve nirvana, because they want to continue to work to relieve the suffering of all sentient beings. She also spoke about the International Network of Engaged Buddhists, those who see engagement with the world and the reduction of suffering as important components of their way of living. These conversations made me realize that I could learn a great deal from an extended exchange of ideas with

Chao-Hwei and that a wider audience—whether Buddhists, secular utilitarians, or just people interested in different ways of thinking about how we ought to live—might also benefit from our dialogue.

We have arranged the dialogues that follow to start with foundational questions about the nature of ethics, which will be a valuable precursor to our discussions of important ethical issues. I was also keen to learn more about some Buddhist concepts, particularly those of karma and nirvana, which are frequently mentioned in the West, but in a way that suggested to me that they had been taken out of their original context; hence, the popular Western understanding of them might not reflect their true sense in the Buddhist tradition. Speaking with Chao-Hwei gave me the opportunity to ask a leading Buddhist scholar, monastic, and activist, how she understands them, and we thought that this discussion would also be a useful preliminary to the later dialogues. Next, we have the dialogue in which Chao-Hwei describes her struggles when seeking equality for female monastics, as that enables readers to know more about her activism. From there, it is easy see a connection with the dialogue about sexuality, and after that we move on to questions relating to abortion and embryo experimentation and then animal welfare, the topic that originally brought us together. The last two dialogues are on issues about taking life: euthanasia and suicide, the death penalty, and killing in war.

Peter Singer
Princeton University
New Jersey, USA

Preface

The Lights That Shone When Our Paths Crossed

The dialogues between Professor Peter Singer and me that make up this book commenced in the Kao-Feng Meditation Forest at the Bodhi Monastery in the deep mountain of Musha in Nantou County, Taiwan, on May 25, 2016. With us was Professor Chang Li-Wen of Fu-Jen Catholic University, who served as our interpreter. Our group left early from the Buddhist Hong-Shi College in Taoyuan and arrived in Musha at noon. The abbot of the Bodhi Monastery, Venerable Hsing-Kuang, and all the monastic members gave us a warm welcome and took outstanding care of us during our stay.

Our dialogues, exploring philosophy and religion, have been through the arduous process of English and Chinese transcription and three different translators. Finally, I found Yuan Shiao-Ching, a professional interpreter with ample Buddhist knowledge to undertake this project. Since then, Peter and I have exchanged ideas and discussed questions critically and carefully via e-mail with Shiao-Ching's assistance, and we collaborated on fine-tuning word choices, proofreading, and editing. Shiao-Ching translated our dialogues in both English and Chinese with precision and paid close attention to our conversation. She has indeed been a valuable collaborative partner in this work.

In my position as an academic administrator at Hsuan Chuang University, I often deal with detail-oriented and extensive work. As a result, I have not always been able to respond to Peter in a timely manner, which caused the whole process to move more slowly than I wished and caused me immense distress. However, Peter has always treated my delays with understanding and graciousness and has regarded the five years we have worked on this dialogue together as an opportunity for our mutual understanding to deespen and our thoughts to mature. I am grateful for his considerate and warm responses.

Peter's philosophical thoughts are carefully organized and reasoned. In addition, he is very gentle and thoughtful in nature. It has always been delightful to be in his presence. Although he has faced sharp criticism due to his philosophy, he remains calm and treats these rebuffs with humor. He advocates for effective altruism and voices for minorities and animals. For him, effective altruism is not an idea that stays on paper but an action to be practically taken in life. To me, he is like a bodhisattva who has sprung from an ancient Buddhist Mahayana sutra and landed gracefully in this world.

During our five-year, ongoing conversation, many misunderstandings and cultural and intellectual differences between our respective theories were clarified through the process of our correspondence. Peter's questions constantly challenged me to think in more depth. Therefore, I believe the person who benefited the most from these dialogues is myself.

The working title of our book was *Meeting of Minds*. Although in the end we changed this to a title that provides more information about the specific nature of our talks and the book's contents, I always liked the phrase "meeting of minds." It reminds me of a sentence from a poem by a modern Chinese poet named Xu Zhi-Mo called "By Chance": "The lights that shone when our paths crossed." Time and again, the encounter between Buddhist philosophy and utilitarianism has shone the clear and bright light of wisdom, which brings me great satisfaction and the incomparable joy of dharma.

Shih Chao-Hwei
Buddhist Hong Shi College
Taiwan

Acknowledgments

The dialogues that follow began in a perfect setting at the Bodhi Monastery in the Kao-Feng Meditation Forest in Taiwan. I am particularly grateful to Hsing-Kuang, the abbot of the monastery, and all the others who made us feel very welcome there. She and others at the monastery provided an audience for our discussions, which continued informally over delicious vegetarian meals.

I especially thank Chang Li-Wen for acting as an interpreter for the in-person dialogues, and Yuan Shiao-Ching for translating the very considerably revised and extended written version of those dialogues that appears here. The translators faced the extraordinarily difficult task of translating not only words but also the concepts they expressed, even when these concepts had no real equivalent in the other philosophical tradition. I believe that their work enabled Chao-Hwei and me to achieve the high degree of mutual comprehension required for any genuine dialogue.

My greatest debt, of course, is to Chao-Hwei herself, for her commitment to take part in this dialogue and her patience and resolution in seeing the dialogue completed, despite her many other commitments. She is the founder of Buddhist Hong-Shi College, and for much of the time we were working on this book, she was also dean of the Faculty of Social Science and chair of the department of religion and culture at Hsuan Chuang University where she teaches ethics. In order to have more time to complete this book, in July 2020 she resigned from these academic director positions. In her commitment to the exchange of ideas, her willingness to have her ideas challenged, and her ability to think for herself, Chao-Hwei shows that she is not only a leading interpreter and practitioner of the Buddhist tradition but also a true philosopher.

Peter Singer

The publication of this book has depended on the tireless and generous help of the following friends and students: Lee Fang-Zhi and the late Hsieh Hui-Luen, who shouldered the expense of translation and publication; Professor Chang Li-Wen, who was responsible for interpretation and English transcription during our actual dialogues; Professor Chang, Dilan Schulte, and Kang Yun-Ling, who each participated in the initial translation; Venerable Hsing-Kuang, who offered the best venue—Bodhi Monastery—for these dialogues; the Buddhist Hong-Shi College, the monastic members of Kao-Feng Meditation Forest, Chang Zhang-De, Lee Yen-Zhi, and Yu Chung-Chao; our team for the Chinese transcription, proofreading, editing, and publication, which includes Venerables Ming-Yi, Yao-Hsing, Hsin-Hao, and Huang Hsiu-Er. We offer our heartfelt gratitude to all of them.

Shih Chao-Hwei

The Buddhist and the Ethicist

Shih Chao-Hwei and Peter Singer together on the
second morning before their dialogues (May 26, 2016)

The conversations in this book began in person at Kao-Feng Meditation Retreat Center, Nantou, Taiwan, in May 2016 and continued in writing for the next five years.

CHAPTER 1

The Foundations of Ethics

SINGER: I'll start with a question about the extent to which Buddhist ethics is utilitarian. As a utilitarian, I hold that whether an act is right or wrong depends ultimately on whether it leads to better consequences than anything else that I could have done. Is that consistent with the Buddhist view? To sharpen the question, I will supplement it by asking another: Are there some things that a Buddhist would never do? Because if there are some things that a Buddhist would never do, even if they had the best consequences, then Buddhism is not utilitarian. For example, Roman Catholics say it's always wrong to intentionally kill an innocent human being, whereas a utilitarian would say, if somehow the only way you could save many innocent human beings from being killed is for you yourself to kill one innocent human being, then—very reluctantly of course—that would be the right thing to do.

CHAO-HWEI: There are two kinds of approaches to such matters. There is, as you have said, the utilitarian perspective, from which the judgment of whether the act is right or wrong is based on the goodness it brings to the majority. On the other hand, you have the approach (deontological ethics) that will judge whether an act is right or wrong based on the Golden

Rule—that is, you will not do to others what you do not want others to do to you.

In many cases the Buddhist approach is very similar to that of utilitarianism because the Buddha often encouraged people to benefit themselves and others. In order to seek a path for all beings to be free from the cycle of birth, aging, sickness, and death, the Buddha gave up his aristocratic rank and worldly enjoyments. He left his palace and took up dharma practice; that is, he became a monk with no possessions, meditating and practicing asceticism. After he reached enlightenment, he continued to travel around and propagate dharma for the sake of others' well-being. Without a doubt, his motivation for practicing and teaching dharma was also pursuing utility.

Nevertheless, sometimes the Golden Rule determines how we make judgments between what is right and what is wrong. Expressions of the Golden Rule seem to be the ultimate source of morality. Something I would not want done to me is something that, in similar circumstances, I will not do to others. So the Buddha's approach does not really make an either/or choice between these two. The example you brought up, in which by reluctantly killing one person we save many innocent lives, is a very tough decision to make. On the basis of the Golden Rule, I can understand that the other person may not want to be killed just to save other innocent lives, and therefore, unless I would be willing to be killed to save other lives, I wouldn't kill the one person even to save many others. Following this thought, again the Buddhist seems to judge whether the act is right or wrong based on the Golden Rule of morality.

Nonetheless, according to the preceding discourse, the Buddha specifically emphasized the goal of alleviating suffering and attaining happiness. He taught meditation as a technique by which we can escape the suffering caused by our desire. He described the benefits of every stage and each level of meditation, and he gave clear guidelines on the ideas one should learn and practice to reach these stages and gain the corresponding benefits. Thus, Buddhism seems to be so close to utilitarianism. Therefore, in my personal opinion, the ethical judgments of Buddhism actually contain the core elements of both utilitarianism and the Golden Rule. If we observe the ethical choices of the general public, individuals often seem to be wavering between the two, because sometimes they will put themselves in others' shoes when they make choices, and at other times they do not exclude the possibility of looking at how to bring about the maximum benefit as a guide for their ethical choices.

The sutras in sacred Buddhist texts can all be categorized as either active or passive. When an issue is more closely related to whether we should refrain from hurting others, then we choose to adopt the second approach—that is, to follow the Golden Rule. And when it comes to sharing resources with others, we can perceive from these texts that there seems to be a stronger suggestion to consider how these resources can bring about the maximum benefit to our shared community.

The Buddhist sutras share two examples regarding the Buddha's previous incarnations that may inspire us to consider whether we should kill the person to save many people. One is about an incident in the life of Shakyamuni Buddha when he was a bodhisattva practicing bodhisattva acts. An eagle was attacking a dove, and the dove came to the Buddha for help. Of course, out of compassion the bodhisattva protected the dove from the eagle. Then the eagle flew down from the sky and argued with the bodhisattva, saying, "Well, I know that out of compassion you want to help the dove, but you are doing a cruel thing to me, because without food I will starve to death."

The bodhisattva thought the eagle had a point, so he decided to cut off a piece of his thigh and give it to the hungry eagle. This story reveals that when we consider maximum benefits for all, rather than sacrificing other innocent beings, it is very likely that a bodhisattva will decide to sacrifice themself instead.

Another example goes like this: In one of his previous lives, Shakyamuni bodhisattva joined a group of five hundred merchants on a ship seeking some precious jewels. Unfortunately, the captain of the ship was a pirate, so he got everybody drunk and was about to steal their possessions. But the bodhisattva stayed awake because he adhered to the nondrinking vow and saw that the pirate captain was ready to kill all five hundred passengers. He realized that not only would the merchants lose their lives and die in pain, but their families would also be devastated. In addition, the captain was going to commit an act so evil that it would lead him to hell. Therefore, out of compassion for the five hundred merchants, their families, and the pirate captain, he decided to push the captain into the sea. He knew that he would have to live with the consequences of such a killing and willingly accepted them. This story reveals that the principle of a bodhisattva act is also based on the maximum possible benefit for the greatest number.

One important difference between this scenario and the one you raised in your question is, of course, that the pirate is not an innocent person. We need to take into consideration the person who is about to be killed to save the other innocent lives and whether this person is evil or innocent. If we are sure that the person who is going to be killed is evil, then it's permissible for the bodhisattva to kill. There is a Chinese expression, "*Da kai sha jei,*" which indicates that a Buddhist disciple, who normally upholds the precept of not killing, has let go of that precept completely and become open to killing in this special situa-

THE FOUNDATIONS OF ETHICS | 5

tion. Of course, the disciple must be very sure that there are no other options. The bodhisattva must also be very merciful when killing because they are very aware of the pain that comes with killing, but they are also aware of the greater pain that will come from not killing, both for the bodhisattva, who will have to live with the consequences, and for the other people who will be killed. So in some circumstances the bodhisattva must choose to just let the person who must be killed go through the suffering of being killed rather than have to cope with the consequences of that person's evil deeds.

SINGER: Thank you for that interesting answer and especially for the story of justifiable killing. First, just to make sure that our readers properly understand the nature of utilitarianism, I must comment on your statement that utilitarianism seeks to maximize the benefit for the majority. That's a common misunderstanding that goes back to a slogan from Jeremy Bentham, the founder of utilitarianism as a systematic approach to ethics and public policy: "The greatest happiness for the greatest number." It's not quite accurate, though, as utilitarianism really tells us to do what will lead to the *greatest possible benefit*, and sometimes this will mean that we should do what will benefit a minority of those affected if that minority will gain a great deal, whereas the majority will only lose a little. A popular objection to utilitarianism is that it would justify the cruel spectacles in the Roman Coliseum, on the grounds that if ten thousand people enjoy watching ten prisoners being torn apart by lions, then that benefits the majority. But the utilitarian would say that even though there are only ten prisoners and ten thousand spectators, the ten prisoners will suffer so greatly that the entertainment of ten thousand still does not outweigh their suffering. That seems right to me.

CHAO-HWEI: It's not only the number but the overall intensity?

SINGER: Yes, that's correct.

CHAO-HWEI: It is completely understandable that the suffering of ten people can outweigh the entertainment of ten thousand; the weighing between the two sides is easy to perceive. I think this example can easily help one to understand the rationality of utilitarianism. I would like to bring up a more difficult choice, one that I believe you know well. We have two trains. One train, full of passengers, has stopped at the station on the wrong track. Then along comes an incoming train. If it continues along the track, it will hit the stationary train, and there will be a lethal collision, killing and injuring many passengers on both trains. You are standing by a railway switch. The only thing you can do is switch the incoming train to a sidetrack. There is no other train on that track, but an innocent child is playing there. If you switch the train onto the sidetrack, the child will be killed, but no one else will be harmed. Am I right in thinking that a utilitarian would decide to switch the train to the sidetrack, so that only the innocent child is killed and not many more people in both trains?

SINGER: Yes, that's correct. The utilitarian would want to minimize the harm, so if there's no other choice, the utilitarian will take the action that will mean the innocent child dies, because that will save many innocent lives.

CHAO-HWEI: I'm asking myself what the person standing by the railway switch would do if they were a Buddhist. It's very likely that they would, like the utilitarian, choose to switch the incoming train to the sidetrack where the innocent child is playing. But as a Buddhist, they would not see this as the right thing to do but as an utterly regrettable thing to do.

SINGER: It's regrettable but still better than the other option.

CHAO-HWEI: I agree.

SINGER: The utilitarian feels that although any decent human being should regret having to make this choice, if it's the choice that will be the most beneficial, then it's still the right choice. It would be wrong not to do it, because then so many more innocent lives would be lost.

CHAO-HWEI: This is a classical dilemma in which we have to make the decision right away, and we have to choose the act that will lead to less harm. But is this the way we want to think about real issues that confront us, where we do not have to decide right away? I would question that because of examples like the following. Normally we would not want to have a recycling and garbage center next door. We'd want to push it as far away as possible until eventually the garbage and recycling center would be in a remote part of the country, near only a minority of the country's population. The public policy makers would feel neither a sense of guilt nor an attack of conscience about that, because to them it was the right decision. A person who follows the Golden Rule approach, however, would think that this is wrong because we are doing to others what we don't want done to us, and therefore it is an injustice.

In Taiwan we recently had a similar discussion about building another nuclear power plant—we have three, and this would have been the fourth. We were constantly told that without a new nuclear power plant, we would very quickly run out of electrical energy. Normally the new nuclear power plant would be built in the countryside where the minority of people live. We need to balance the two approaches when we discuss such issues. In this case, eventually our protest stopped the fourth plant halfway through its construction. We succeeded in stopping it because we had the support of people who believe that we shouldn't do to others what we wouldn't want done to us, even though they are a minority of the population of Taiwan. Without appealing to this principle, it is very likely that we would have had the fourth nuclear power plant installed in that remote country area, and then eventually we could have a fifth and a sixth.

I have discovered an interesting phenomenon: in Taiwan, social movements like the one opposing the construction of the fourth power plant normally emphasize justice, and public policy makers usually emphasize the greatest benefits. In addition, if social activists who emphasize justice later rise to prominence to become makers of public policy, they may experience a mindset change as their roles shift. When they have to evaluate different policies, they often become utilitarians. So it's not *either* justice or utilitarianism that has the whole truth about right or wrong; rather, there should be this constant debate to balance out the two sides.

SINGER: It's true that when people have a strong commitment to justice, they can bring about a better result than would be possible if they did not have such a commitment. This is particularly likely to be the case if the commitment is to an understanding of justice that has special concern for the poorest and most disadvantaged section of the community. These are the people who are most likely to be exploited by the ruling elite and, as your examples show, are more likely to have undesirable things like garbage dumps and nuclear power plants located in their neighborhoods. When such issues are being discussed, utilitarianism often doesn't give a precise answer to what the net sum of all the costs and benefits are, so those in power can make use of a utilitarian calculation, rigged to point to the outcome they prefer, to defend decisions that impose burdens on the powerless.

I want to stress that very often these decisions are not justifiable in utilitarian terms, but that is difficult to prove, and if the decision is convenient for the majority, then the majority will not examine the utilitarian calculations too closely. In these situations, an appeal to the majority's sense of justice can be a good way of resisting this tendency of utilitarianism to be misused.

CHAO-HWEI: To clarify, you're saying that we need to balance the two principles?

SINGER: No, that's not exactly what I'm saying. I think that when our sense of justice tells us that something is unjust, we should treat that as a warning sign that says, "Go back and check the utilitarian calculations. Maybe this is one of those cases where you're ignoring the interests of people who can't speak up for themselves."

CHAO-HWEI: I can agree with that.

SINGER: Very good. I also have a comment about the use of the Golden Rule. You contrasted an appeal to utilitarianism with an appeal to the Golden Rule, but I don't think the contrast is as clear as you suggested. If we have only two people involved— let's say, you and me—then I might ask myself, "Would I like that if it were done to me?" If the answer is no, then I should not do it to you. But there are many situations in which there are more than two people involved, often many more. You just gave us one such situation, in the example of the train that would collide with the train full of passengers, unless it were switched to the track on which the child was playing. In situations in which many people are involved, it might be right to do to one or even several people something that, if I were in that person's position, I would not want done to me.

Before you gave us the example of building the fourth nuclear power plant, you also mentioned the problem of situating a recycling and garbage disposal plant. We need to dispose of our garbage somehow, and it's good to recycle as much of it as possible, thus saving waste and conserving energy. This has to take place somewhere, and although we can try to reduce offensive odors and problems of flies and rodents, it may not be possible to eliminate these problems entirely. If the country does not have any completely vacant places with no people, or if the only such places are wildernesses that should be preserved to protect biodiversity or for their scenic value, then there are bound to be people who are disadvantaged by living near the recycling and garbage disposal plant.

If I were living near a proposed site for that plant and someone were to ask, "Would you like to have this recycling plant next to you?" I would say, "No." Should I then follow the Golden Rule and say that since I would not want this plant next to me, I should not support a proposal to have it near anyone who objects to it? That might make it impossible to put it anywhere at all. That would not be the best outcome. We should locate it where it will cause the least harm. In considering where that is, we should give everyone's interest equal weight. It's possible that will mean that it should be built near my own home. But it is also possible that this would be bad for many more people than if it were located far away from my home. We should do our best to judge impartially between these options. It is possible to see that as the right thing to do—both on the utilitarian approach and also on the Golden Rule approach—because it is the outcome you get if you put yourself in the situation of *all* the people affected by the decision. The philosopher R. M. Hare, who was my teacher when I was a student at the University of Oxford, proposed that we can get the right answer to such questions by asking ourselves what outcome we would prefer if we were going to live the lives of each and every individual affected by the decision.[1] That question brings together the Golden Rule and utilitarianism.

CHAO-HWEI: So you are saying that the Golden Rule applies to all the others involved, is that right?

SINGER: Exactly. I have to consider the interests of all the people involved. So when I am asking, "Would I like this if I were in A's place?" I have to come to an answer. Then I have to ask it over and over again for B and for C and for each person affected.

CHAO-HWEI: I see. It makes sense to make a rational decision in this way. Thank you for offering a more comprehensive view of utilitarianism, which improves my understanding about all aspects of consideration included in this approach. One takes into consideration all the parties involved, and one must also feel for all the people. In that way, compassion is put into consideration. From the perspective of Buddhism, compassion is a feeling that is the basis for morality. Compassion should be applied to everybody, not only to a single individual. It's a process in which the final decision involves not only weighing or rationally calculating the amounts of happiness and suffering but also one in which this kind of compassion is at work. That means it is a process that involves both reason and emotion, so the process eventually leads to bringing about the best consequences for everyone.

SINGER: The Buddhist view of compassion as a feeling that is the basis of morality sounds very like the eighteenth-century Scottish philosophers, especially Adam Smith and David Hume. They also thought that morality is based on feelings and gave sympathy—by which they meant something similar to what we have been calling compassion—a central role.

That brings us to the next question I wanted to talk about. I am frequently asked, usually by Christians or other theists, "Where do you think ethics comes from?" Believers in the monotheistic religions often ask that question because they think that ethics comes from God. In the simplest version, they believe that God gave the Ten Commandments to Moses. Not all theists are as crude as that, of course, but in some way, they think that God is the foundation of ethics, and they have trouble imagining where else ethics could come from or why anyone would have sufficient reason to do what is right if that should be contrary to their own interests. I don't think ethics comes from God—that's obvious, because I am an atheist—but the nature of ethics and what foundations, if any, it can have is a much-debated topic in philosophy. I am interested to learn how a Buddhist would answer that question.

CHAO-HWEI: It is possible that if a person believes that ethics comes from God and then ceases to believe in God, that person will begin to act immorally. Or at least, the kind of moral life that was central to the person's way of living when that person believed in God would no longer be central to their life once they became an atheist. But although this is possible, what we observe all around us indicates that belief in God is not necessary for living a morally good life.

Take Christianity, for example. When the religion spread to Greece, it had to interact and adjust to the Greek discourse about reason. Therefore, it had to admit that people who could reason are capable of making moral judgments even if they are not theists. Later, Thomas Aquinas said that non-Christians could also possess four cardinal virtues—prudence (or wisdom), justice, fortitude (or courage), and temperance. However, when one is not a Christian, it is impossible to have supernatural virtues—faith, hope, and love (or charity). He even further explained that the four cardinal virtues are created by God. As a result, he resolved the conflict between the theological belief that God is the root of ethics and the practical condition that even non-Christians can live ethically.

How would a Buddhist look at this issue? As Buddhists, we say that we cannot verify that God created the world or that God saves the world, as this belief is beyond our experience. So either you resort to faith, or you resort to imagination. That leads to the fact that those who believe will believe, and those who do not believe will not believe. But we cannot claim that those who do not believe are immoral, because in reality we see moral people who are nonbelievers. From the Buddhist perspective, we agree that there are these natural rules. If we use a Buddhist term to describe these rules, it would be the principle of *interdependent origination*, the myriad results that arise from various causes and conditions. The Buddha is not the creator of all this, but he realized that everything is a result of multiple causes and influences that combine with and condition each other.

At first glance, this idea of interdependent origination and its connection with living ethically is more difficult to articulate than the Christian account of morality. Christian theory holds that morality comes from God because God represents the qualities of love, and if one is connected to God, one is connected to love; therefore, one is able to love one's neighbors as well as one's foes. This deduction can be easily understood. But Christians will eventually have to confront the problem: is it possible to prove that God exists? Since the existence of God is a premise that cannot be verified, the inference that God loves humans and humans love God in return seems to be based on a weak theoretical foundation. At the same time, Buddhism does not argue with others about things that cannot be verified.

SINGER: So Buddhism has no position on the existence of God? It is neither for it nor against it, is that right?

CHAO-HWEI: Buddhism teaches that this world is not created by a single creator. The world is working in interdependent coordination. But Buddhism will not use its energies to argue for or against the existence of God. Just simply understanding or being aware of the phenomenon that things appear and disappear, based on these causes or conditions, or those causes and conditions—all of which is described as *interdependent coordination*—just observing all this does not tell us what is wrong or right. If you are in the forest and you see a lion bite off the head of a goat, eat its meat, and drink its blood, you cannot tell if this is right or wrong. This reflects the law of the universe—the weak are devoured by the strong. But how can you judge whether the lion is right or the goat is wrong? This is just something that happens constantly.

At the same time, we are aware of the psychological principle of having compassion toward those who are suffering and anguished in the natural world; that is, a person can feel compassion when they see another being in pain. This can even be observed in other species. We observe these phenomena with the cats and dogs in our college. For example, one day a rescued stray cat in our Buddhist college accidently fell into a drainage ditch. A dog saw this and started barking. His ceaseless barking drew our attention, and we all came out and then saw the trapped, injured cat. We would not have discovered that without the dog's help. So the working of compassion can be observed with nonhuman animals too, and it can be cross-species.

In Greek philosophy it seems to have been widely accepted that the distinction between right and wrong is made by reason, which is capable of grasping the natural moral law. In accordance with this view, it is not wrong to kill animals since they are classified as nonrational beings. As a result, they are not included in moral concerns. In the East, by contrast, when we talk about natural moral law, we place more emphasis on the capacity to feel for other species. Since the foundation of ethics or morality comes from our capacity to feel for the other, including other species, then it can transcend the interspecies boundary. Therefore, moral concern is not limited by the capacity to reason nor—as Immanuel Kant thought—to be self-conscious, which also has its basis in reason.

SINGER: I understand that the Buddhist view is that the foundations of ethics lie in our nature and our capacity to experience compassion for others. Some philosophers argue that you can't just move from the fact that this is in our nature to the moral judgment that this is what we ought to do. A further step is, they say, necessary: we must endorse certain elements of our nature. We cannot just hold that whatever is natural to us is right, because of course there are other elements of our nature, such as hatred of outsiders, that we would not think right at all. If we cannot simply appeal to nature, how do we reach the judgment that we endorse compassion for those beings who are suffering, but we refuse to endorse hatred of outsiders? My current position is that at this point, reason has to play a role. Certainly compassion is an important motivation, but if we want to say not just that this is how we *are*, but that it is also how we *ought* to be, then we have to say that there's some kind of truth in our saying that it is better for us to act out of our compassion than to act out of xenophobia. We have to say that there is something like a self-evident perception, or perhaps "intuition" (that is the word that Henry Sidgwick uses) that enables us to see that relieving suffering is good and increasing suffering is bad. This is, if you like, a truth about the universe: that it is better to decrease suffering than to increase it.

CHAO-HWEI: We need to take into consideration reason, emotion, and also will. When I said that morality is based on feelings and compassion, I did not exclude reason. Hume once said that reason is the slave of passions. Hume's observation is similar to the experiences that Buddhism describes. Among will and reason and passion, which one is more dominant? When the Buddhist analyzes the three elements that affect how the mind works, normally passion will be the first, then it will be followed by the working of reason and then the operation of will. Normally, passion seems to be more dominant, reason will be involved in planning how we are to satisfy the passion, and we apply our will in order to carry out the plan.

Sometimes an emotion arises, and before reason can be effective, willpower brings out actions that correspond to the emotion. Therefore, it is described in the Samyukta Agama (an early collection of Chinese Buddhist texts): When there is a touch, immediately there is a sensation; the sensation then triggers the thinking process, which leads to the creation of thoughts.[2] This means that when sense organs, scenarios, and the distinguishing functions from these organs interact, sensations are created, and willpower is developed. Reasoning occurs last. This is common for both human and animal instincts. They can hardly be controlled by reason. Christianity realizes that the impulse derived from this instinct often goes against the response offered by reason, thus Christians call it a sin. On the other hand, Buddhism does not see this as a sin, but merely a physical and mental function that is neither good nor bad. However, Buddhism does want to remind people that simply allowing instinct to lead our ways and satisfy our greed represents a lack of wisdom. In Buddhism this is called ignorance, which will bring suffering and pressure to one's body and mind. Hence, while Christians are tormented by the feeling of guilt, Buddhists feel suffering deeply.

The function of reason is to direct the passion in a more constructive direction. In Buddhism, when describing human beings or all beings, the term *sentient beings* is often used because *sentient* means "to be conscious of feelings." On the other hand, when we try to describe an enlightened one, we call it *prajna*, which means "transcendent wisdom." Only when one attains this level of wisdom can one behave beyond the dominance of instinct that culminates in the perfection of kindness. So, yes, of course, reason plays a very important role.

SINGER: Okay, but which comes first? The way you said that now, it sounds like reason is the leader.

CHAO-HWEI: No, no. Fundamentally, passion is the one that takes the initiative.

SINGER: So we start with passion, but then reason comes in. Let me give you an example. I am walking with my granddaughter, and we pass a toy shop that has in the window an expensive new toy that she would like. She asks me to buy it for her, but I tell her, "No, I cannot buy you that toy, although I love you very much. You have a lot of toys already, and there are other children elsewhere in the world who do not even have enough to eat, and I should give the money to help those children." Now my passion goes with my granddaughter, and I don't feel much for the children in extreme poverty who will be helped by my donation to a charity—I don't even know who they are. Nevertheless, this is the reason why I do not spend more on my grandchildren.

CHAO-HWEI: The passion or the emotion that is the basis of our morality is not a kind of self-love that is directed to the self or directed in the way of self-interest. It is the compassion we develop for the other that is the foundation of our morality and ethics.

SINGER: But how do we get to this more universal compassion without the appeal to reason?

CHAO-HWEI: It's not either/or between reason and emotion.

SINGER: Perhaps I have become confused because you said that the Buddhist view is the same as Hume's view that reason is the slave of the passions. My understanding of Hume's view—supported by the very strong word that he uses, *slave*—is that passion is completely dominant over reason, to such an extent that the role of reason is limited to serving the passions, to helping them to be satisfied.

CHAO-HWEI: I do not think we need to exclude reason. When we consider whether we want to further our own self-love or self-interest, or whether we want to extend the self-love to be redirected toward others so that we benefit them, reason plays a very important role.

When we discuss the respective roles of passion and reason, we cannot start by talking about the enlightened ones, or the holy people called bodhisattvas. We should talk about ordinary people. Otherwise we would talk about a lot of things that would only be applicable to bodhisattvas. If we observe bodhisattvas, we will discover a principle—the more selfless their emotions are, the stronger their compassion or empathy for others is. When their emotions are guided by reason to act altruistically, their service to others is more powerful. In a different way, reason completes the strong, purified, selfless passion of bodhisattvas to benefit others.

SINGER: Would it be true to say that the difference between the bodhisattva and the ordinary person is not just that the bodhisattva feels stronger compassion but also that the bodhisattva makes more use of reason?

CHAO-HWEI: Yes, that is why the Buddha describes the enlightened one as equipped with both compassion and wisdom, which represent the completion of both emotion and reason.

SINGER: Thank you, that gives me a better understanding of the Buddhist view, and it is closer to my own current view.

I used to be more a follower of Hume, but now I am closer to Sidgwick, who thought that reason plays a greater role than Hume was willing to grant it.

CHAO-HWEI: Perhaps I should offer another thought. People often assume that these discussions are about human nature. They think we are inquiring into whether compassion for others is innate or has to be learned. We wouldn't use the term *nature* or *innate nature*, and we would never say that we ought to follow nature or that nature is best, because it would lead to the fallacy of naturalism. According to the Buddhist understanding, nothing can exist permanently and function independently. The former is called impermanence, whereas the latter is called selflessness. The body and mind seem independent, which creates a misunderstanding of a self-existent "I." Actually, neither the mental nor the physical part can exist without the codependence of causes or conditions. Therefore, the body and mind are constantly in the process of experiencing changes. We can even state that no phenomenon can come into existence without interdependent origination, whether it involves sentient beings or nonsentient beings.

A follower of Confucius would argue that compassion is born with you, that it is part of your nature; a Buddhist would deny that and instead say that compassion is not part of one's nature but rather a phenomenon arising from dependent origination. The Buddhist way of describing this is that we need certain factors for compassion to work and take effect. We need a person with a capacity for compassion, who is equipped with an awareness of others' pain; at the same time, we need a situation that will give rise to the compassion in this person. Only then will the person have compassion. In other words, compassion is

TH E FOUN DATIONS OF ETHICS | 21

not a quality that always exists or exists independently. It takes some other causes and conditions for one to have compassion.

SINGER: Very good, that also helps me to have a better understanding of the Buddhist position on these questions.

CHAPTER 2

Key Buddhist Concepts: Karma and Nirvana

SINGER: Now we come to the concept of karma. This term is so familiar in the West that you can buy T-shirts with definitions of karma on them. I recently saw one that said, "Karma is using the last piece of toilet paper without replacing the roll and then being the next person who uses the bathroom." No doubt this is a silly trivialization of the Buddhist understanding of the term, but I would like to get the correct understanding from you. How do Buddhists understand karma? In particular, do Buddhists believe that people who do bad things will suffer from what they do?

CHAO-HWEI: I really cannot see any connection between the true meaning of karma and this quote you saw on the T-shirt. The word *karma* comes from Sanskrit. Its root *kr* means "operation" or "in process." Deeds of body, speech, and mind leave traces in this world, and these traces become manifest at an appropriate time when causes and conditions have ripened. In fact, the concept of karma was mentioned in the ancient Sanskrit texts, the Upanishads. In these texts, it is said of karma that "Atman (self) does, and I receive the consequences." So the idea of karma was already quite developed in ancient India. This idea in the Upanishads is subverting the Brahmin belief that humans please the gods and spirits through worship and prayers, and through this they gain joy and happiness. Let me briefly explain how the idea of karma originated in India and how it has developed in Buddhism.

Brahmanism emphasizes the power of the other, of the divine being, to reward us, whereas the idea of karma emphasizes that everyone should be responsible for creating their own happiness rather than worshipping and expecting to get happiness from God/gods. The caste system associated with Brahmanism classifies people and has a select group of individuals who are the chosen ones and others who are the excluded group. It is said that the Brahmin caste is born from the mouth of Brahma, the divine creator, while the other castes come from other parts. The Kshatriya (warrior) caste comes from his belly button; the Vaishya caste (whose livelihood is agriculture or business), from his knees; and the Sudra, the lowest ranked of the four castes, from the bottom of his feet. Only the first three castes can be reincarnated. The last type cannot be reborn; they have only one life. The caste system was originally a categorization of different occupations. Brahmins believed they had the endorsement of holy texts, and Brahmanism put in place a hierarchy that contrasted noble versus baseborn, upper versus lower class, unsoiled versus befouled; it stigmatized the lowest caste to the point that its members would never stand a chance in life.

The view of the Upanishads is more progressive. They point out that the deity does not decide whether we are happy or not, nor whether we are noble or not. Therefore, according to this description, our happiness comes from our own doing, our karma. This was, as previously mentioned, already a very widely accepted idea in India before the Buddha. People believed that there is a continuing self, "Atman," an "I" that is doing all the deeds and receiving the consequences of those deeds; that is, the karma, from one life to the next, the connection continues. The Buddha accepted that our deeds do have karmic consequences, but he did not accept the concept of Atman—a continuing, permanent, and independent self. The Buddha said there is not an Atman who continues to exist because the body, the mind, and all the other causes and conditions are constantly changing their combinations. So the contribution of Buddhism to the idea of karma is to allow for possibilities of change. Even though a person may previously have done many bad deeds, if the person starts to make changes, then the consequences will be different.

There is a common misunderstanding about karma that says whatever we are experiencing now can be traced back to an earlier life from which we have been reincarnated and so has already been determined by our behavior in that previous life. This view is a form of fatalism. It rationalizes and justifies present circumstances with an explanation about how the past determines the present. That misunderstanding of karma ignores the possibilities of change in the present and can be an obstacle to efforts to transform oneself and one's circumstances, as well as a deterrent to attempts to reform society. Opposed to this, the Buddha argued that if fatalism were true, then killing could be justified, because fatalists would argue, "A is killed by B because A had killed B in the past." This viewpoint creates a second harm to the victim. In Indian Buddhist communities like Nagaloka, which is led by Lokamitra, Dalit teachers and students are referred to as "untouchables" and do not like to hear the word *karma*, because it seems that the idea of karma justifies their status as untouchables in this life.

Given this situation, should they just accept the caste system and discrimination and suppression derived from this system, or is there any room for reforming the system and striving for better human rights?

We can think of karma as having three aspects: (1) previous causes, (2) current conditions, (3) and communal karma. First, we can consider the possibility that the past exercises a continuing influence on the present. Our previous speech and actions have an influence on our future. Second, our present ethical choices also contribute to the formation of karma; they will have consequences. Karma therefore should not be seen as fatalism, nor as a reason for giving up the attempt to create a brighter, more positive future here and now—that applies to everyone.

In Buddhism, there is a third type of karmic influence that is communal. It is seen as a common tendency that will create shared circumstances for a group of people over a period of time, and the people must face these circumstances together. If, for example, a city or country is stricken by some natural disaster, we may say that this is the result of communal karma. To avoid a misunderstanding here, we should note that the shared tendencies or behavior of a group of people could result in disasters that might only affect some disadvantaged or minority group. Even though these disadvantaged or minority groups are the small population who suffer the consequences of the shared behavior, we cannot claim that this is their karma.

Imagine, for example, that we have a group of people in Taiwan who want cheap electricity, so they support the building of a new nuclear power plant. Eventually there is a disaster, but the brunt of the disaster falls only on the people living close to that plant. It would be a misreading of the idea of communal karma to say that this specific group of people is suffering the negative karma from their own actions only. The karma of this disaster is cocreated by all of those who wanted cheap electricity. The specific group of people who happen to live near the plant, on the contrary, are often against nuclear power. So when we have an ongoing discussion about karma, there are three aspects that need to be taken into consideration: deeds in the past (previous causes), the current actions (present conditions), and finally the shared social climate (communal karma). We have to examine the causes and consequences of events from the aforementioned three aspects.

SINGER: I don't see the way you explain karma as contrary to the modern scientific view of the world that I hold. On the popular conception of karma, at least in the West, if you do something wrong, then your wrongdoing is bound to harm you. I don't think that idea accords with our observations of the way the world works. But if I understand you correctly, in the Buddhist understanding of karma, it's not inevitable that those who engage in wrongdoing will suffer from the consequences of their actions. As the example of the nuclear power plant shows, it might be that the worst consequences are suffered by people who were opposed to the building of the plant, whereas those who supported its construction but live far from it escape relatively unscathed.

CHAO-HWEI: The phenomenon regarding negative actions begetting negative results can be observed in daily life. For example, if a person mistreats others, it will bring about negative treatment on the doer.

SINGER: It always will?

CHAO-HWEI: When people are unfriendly to others, normally others will not be friendly to them. We see this in most cases. It is possible that even though A is unfriendly to B, B could be a well-cultivated person who consciously and reasonably chooses to ignore the unfriendly treatment and continues to show friendliness to A. From that point onward, there will be a difference in the interaction between A and B. The most positive contribution that the theory of karma makes is to create an ideal scenario in which one helps others selflessly and wholeheartedly. Even if one cannot be selfless, or one does good things out of self-interest hoping to get positive results, at least one does not perform any harmful acts. Karma tells us that we should do more good deeds so we can enjoy the consequences of these good deeds. Does that answer your question?

SINGER: Partly, but I still want to know how inevitable it is, from a Buddhist point of view, that wrongdoing will harm the wrongdoer. We can all think of examples of criminals who have successfully pulled off a big robbery, or defrauded a company, or accepted bribes, and they get away with it and live the rest of their lives in luxury. If we believe that death is the end of existence and there is no afterlife, then these wrongdoers do not appear to suffer from their wrongdoing. They have no comeuppance. So where is the karma there? Are our observations of the lives of people like that contrary to the theory of karma, or does this really have nothing to do with karma as a Buddhist would understand it?

CHAO-HWEI: Regarding the fruition of conduct, this can be divided into three categories. The first is about the fruition of this current life and this moment. The second is about the future. The third one takes more time to ripen after countless future lifetimes. So to talk about fruition means to talk about past, current, and future lives. This is what is commonly referred to in Buddhism as "the theory of causal efficacy of the three times—past, present, and future."

SINGER: *Our* future lives? Or any other lives that come after? Because if you mean *our* future lives—that is, the lives of the wrongdoers—then this seems to contradict what I thought you said earlier, that there is no official Buddhist doctrine that says there is an afterlife, and whether or not there is an afterlife is a matter of private belief.

CHAO-HWEI: What I meant was that for phenomena that we cannot experience, such as the existence of God, the believers will always believe and nonbelievers won't. One's only resources are belief and imagination. Nevertheless, part of the consequences of karma can be experienced in one's present life. However, some karma does not have immediate fruition because causes and conditions have not ripened, so the fruition of that karma can only happen in future lives. This is the part that common people have no experience of; in Buddhist scriptures, it is mentioned that past lives and future lives cannot be experienced by the general public.

I wanted to push further against the assumption that forms the basis of your question. How do we prove that these criminals you describe . . . let's say, a bank robber gets away with their crime and really enjoys the rest of their life in luxury. How do we account for such an event without considering the future lives? If we do not talk about the next life and lives that come after that, wouldn't it make it even more infuriating to see this criminal enjoying their opulent life? So comparatively, even if this wrongdoer escapes the punishment of the law, it makes us feel better to know that maybe in a future life this criminal would have to accept the consequences of their actions. Especially in the Eastern world, if you are aware of the possibility that this wrongdoer could receive the consequences of their wrongdoing, it offers a sense of balance. In terms of consolation, when A does bad deeds that harm B, if B is aware that A might suffer from this in a future life, B's perturbation, hatred, and dejection may be somewhat relieved.

SINGER: Yes, but that would depend on how plausible we think it is that there is a next life.

CHAO-HWEI: Well, without the theory of karma, it is even more difficult to talk about consequences, although when we come to the topic of future lives, it is unverifiable. The way the Buddha approached this was he would not try to persuade people to accept the concept of karma and its consequences. On the other hand, if there were practitioners willing to really experience or perceive the actual working of karmic causative consequences, he would encourage them to cultivate and deepen their practice so they would be more acutely alert, sensitive, and aware. It would then be possible to perceive how certain acts lead to certain consequences. When a thought arose, they would immediately know the consequences. This was not achieved through imagination or speculation, but sufficiently sensitive practitioners could actually see these consequences.

To make this a little more understandable, consider economists who are able to predict future trends based on data about past economic trends and the current economic situation. They use this information to make inferences. In a similar manner, meditators cultivate their sensitivity to the extent that they can observe their stream of thoughts and know what consequences these thoughts will have. For example, in our last snack break, we had a plate of corn, right? At the sight of it, I knew that it would be delicious, but my stomach started to have a reaction, and it informed me if I ate the corn, it would not be easy for me to digest. Consequently, my mind would start to feel blurred during our next dialogue due to the corn's effect on my digestion, so I stopped myself from eating it. That is an illustration of how it works. If practitioners cultivate their understanding, they will have factual visualizations that all wrongdoings actually lead to unfortunate and negative results. Furthermore, even a vicious thought could cause some parts of their bodies extreme discomfort, and they would not want to experience bad things, hence they would avoid any kind of wrongdoing.

SINGER: Thank you, I now have a much better sense of what you mean by "karma." May I now ask you about another Buddhist term that is well-known in the West but which I am not sure that I understand correctly? (Or if I do, then perhaps we have a deep disagreement in values.) If one looks at my work—whether it is focused on the way we treat animals, on the plight of those in extreme poverty, or on the legalization of euthanasia—it is possible to see the common thread as preventing unnecessary suffering. Whether that suffering is the suffering of animals in factory farms, of humans living in extreme poverty, or of terminally ill patients who want to die at a time of their own choosing, if we fail to prevent it when we could easily do so, I think we are not acting ethically. As that suggests, I regard suffering as a bad thing; indeed, as the most obvious example of something that, taken in and of itself, is bad and should be prevented where that is possible and where preventing it does not have other bad consequences. Conversely, for me, happiness is a good thing, a positive value that can counterbalance suffering.

Yet I have read that for Buddhists, the ultimate goal is nirvana, which is release from the cycle of life. That is, of course, a release from suffering, but it would also seem to be a release from happiness. I am puzzled by this idea, which seems to me to be one-sided. I take the ultimate goal to be, not release from the cycle of life, but a better life for everyone. To bring that about, we need to change the circumstances of life so there is less suffering and more happiness and so continuing to live is a positive experience for all beings and therefore good. If we can achieve such a world, why would we wish to escape life? But perhaps I have been misinformed about the Buddhist view on this, and if that is the case, I am eager to learn from you.

CHAO-HWEI: The Buddha adjusted his teachings based on those with whom he was interacting. For the majority of people, it is true that the goal of the Buddha's teachings is to increase happiness and reduce suffering, and for the general populace, the prospect of living longer implies that we have a greater potential to increase happiness and joy. So when the Buddha taught people, he didn't talk about nirvana right away. Instead, he promoted happiness in this life and how to get more happiness in future lives.

Once a young Brahmin, a member of India's highest caste, came to the Buddha and asked, "How do I enhance my happiness in this present life?" The Buddha offered him concrete advice: "First, you need to have sufficient professional capability so that you can have a decent career. Second, you need to guard your wealth and fortune well. To do this you have to make good friends, so that you will not become corrupted by the influence of bad friends. You need to strike a balance between your income and your expenses." The Brahmin then went on to ask, "How can I promote or enhance my happiness in future lives?" The Buddha responded, "Number one, you have to believe that your good or evil deeds will bring consequences. Number two, if you are able to share all the resources you have now, then you will never lack resources in future lives. Number three, you must restrain your behaviors so that you don't harm other beings. Number four, use your wisdom to tell good from evil and right from wrong."

From this answer we can understand that the Buddha taught based on the distinct temperament of individual students. He did not offer standard answers to everyone. Even though the Buddha could not use languages to teach animals the aforementioned principles, he would teach human beings to treat animals and the environment well. As you can see, the core of the Buddha's teaching is to eliminate suffering and attain more happiness. Out of respect for the instinct of sentient beings to grow and survive, the Buddha taught people to respect life and not to kill.

Now I must explain the importance of the cultivation of awareness—and by *awareness*, I mean our perception, our ability to be aware of the body, mind, and circumstances. The deeper our capacities of awareness are, the better able we are to see things as they are and realize that even in happiness there are elements of suffering. It's very easy to understand physical pain and suffering; that's obvious. Less obvious is the mental suffering brought by the constant changing and impermanence of the body, mind, and circumstances. Yes, impermanence also includes the constant changes of mind. When we are eating a dish we like, for example, the first bite will be very tasty, and we feel happiness, but after the fourth or fifth bite, the level of our happiness declines; we are neither unhappy nor happy. If you are asked to finish the food on the plate all at once, you might struggle by the end. Actually, the flavor of this dish remains unchanged, but our feelings start with enjoyment, move to neutral, and then turn into suffering. The constant changes of the mind and body will affect how we respond to the same source of happiness.

Thus, we are constantly looking outside ourselves, at the external world, for new and different things that will bring us happiness. The Buddha reminds us that there is a limit to the degree of happiness that these external things will bring us. He also teaches us to look inward to deepen our internal experiences. One often pursues happiness through sensual satisfaction, yet this happiness will result in two possibilities. One is that, with repetition, we become numb to the stimuli; the other is that we will seek to enhance the intensity of the stimuli. When we deepen awareness of our experiences, we realize that the happiness we believe we enjoy actually turns to suffering because we are more and more dependent on sensual pleasures.

The Buddha also teaches that we can elevate our happiness to another level. For instance, before our meal at the dinner table last night, we chanted the following prayer: "When eating our meals, we hope that all sentient beings can delight in the joy of meditation and be filled with the joy of dharma." This was meant to express gratitude to those who donated and prepared our meal, which satisfied our appetite and was delicious. At the same time, we wished that all beings could enjoy such a pleasure. Following that, we wished that all beings would attain another level of happiness beyond sensual pleasure. This is a kind of joy that comes from having a tranquil and focused mind, which is what we refer to as *dhyana*, or "meditative absorption," a happiness that comes from the mind.

There are four levels of dhyana, and the enjoyment of the body and mind deepens at each level. When one reaches the first level, one will no longer feel pain. Even if you cut the person, they will not feel pain. This individual attains a state of tranquility and joy that's reached when one is beyond desires. When one reaches the second dhyana, the fluctuations of the mind's exertions with streams of thoughts slows down, and the thought process becomes extremely calm. This is an even more serene state for the body and mind. When one enters the third dhyana, even the joyful fluctuations of the mind cease, and there is only an extreme calmness of the body, as if every pore relaxes, opens, and becomes featherlight. At the fourth dhyana, the breathing stops, and all bodily sensations cease.

So it is not that the Buddha does not talk about happiness. He just offers what individuals need according to their aptitude. Different people enjoy different types of happiness. Finally, they will be filled with the joy of dharma from realizing the truth of all phenomena.

SINGER: Let me see if I understand this. Certainly, I agree with a lot that was said here, such as how sometimes mere sensual pleasures become jaded. We can seek deeper pleasures, and we can train the mind to experience these more fully. This all makes sense, and I share the values that lie behind these claims. They seem to me to be wise observations about human nature and what brings us happiness. But it became a little puzzling when you described the four stages of the dhyana. I could see the progress from the first to the second, and possibly to the third, but then in the fourth, sensation is lost and breathing stops; this sounds like a bad thing. When you have reached the stage when you are filled with joy and happiness, would it not be better to maintain that stage? Why would we want to stop these sensations? If breathing stops, presumably life stops as well, or at least physical life stops. So from the utilitarian perspective,

I would say it is wonderful that you can reach these first three stages, but why would you want to go further?

CHAO-HWEI: In talking about worldly enjoyment, the Buddha often said the third dhyana offers as much mundane joy as possible. But when the practitioner continues to practice, they will be able to experience that even breathing itself is, in a way, a burden. At the same time, they will be able to see the existence of the body is, in and of itself, heavy. The serenity and calmness that one experienced in the previous stage is still considered heavy in this stage. When your meditation advances, you will be able to let go of this attachment to the body and the happiness attained in the third level. Then you can be liberated further and attain the ultimate and pure state of mind that is extremely tranquil. That is why we want to enter the fourth dhyana state, because it provides the easiest access to enlightenment.

SINGER: I'm still not sure why enlightenment is a goal, and even the supreme goal, above happiness.

CHAO-HWEI: Let's talk about an expression in Chinese Buddhism: "A person is filled with the joy of dharma." In other words, we might say that a person is filled with the happiness that comes from the realization of truth. As practitioners go deeper, they will unavoidably witness the phenomenon of the disturbance of the body and mind, which is centered on an issue called "self-love" in Buddhism. This is an attachment derived from instinct, and it drives human beings to continue developing and seeking enjoyment from sensations. In addition, it resists any threat that will terminate our lives. This strong attachment that originates from self-love cannot be stopped by rationality due to its deep-rooted connection with the survival instinct. If we are not able to let go of this self-love or self-attachment, eventually we will have to deal with the suffering accompanying the birth and cessation of any impermanent phenomena. For example, we have to be separated from our loved ones eventually; we might not always receive what we want; and we will all unavoidably face aging, sickness, and death, which are natural phenomena like the operation of the universe, the changing of the four seasons, and the sunrise and sunset. Because of our self-love, we struggle to see these events like other natural phenomena and observe the impermanence of the body and mind. The pain of our bodies or the sorrow of our souls can become unbearable. We even have a hard time seeing the end of our lives with ease and are unable to treat it as naturally as a leaf falling from a tree.

This is why the Buddha wanted to teach us to cultivate a deep meditative state. When we attain meditative insight, we will be able to personally experience and understand our bodies and our strong attachment to them, which is an illusion based on self-love. The body is just a relatively stable existence. However, the body's cells are like ocean foam gathered and dispersed in an instant; so are our thoughts. If we are able to develop meditative insight and see this, we will realize that there is nothing to be attached to. Thus, we will be able to let go of the strong grasping of self-love and regard our death with ease, just as we see foliage fall from a tree.

When a person proves the truth with their own experience, they will be filled with the joy of dharma. This practitioner has clear insight about the operation of their body and mind, even if the body is relatively stable, and they will stop perceiving it as "I." This realization then terminates the suffering that normally occurs when one experiences changes or even the body and mind's termination. In Buddhist scriptures, when Buddhist practitioners are enlightened, the experience is described as follows: "The only thing I see is the operation of dharma, not the fluctuations of my own emotions." This experience is even more remarkable than the serenity one experiences in meditative absorption. Therefore, in the Buddhist system, the practice of meditation is a tool to help oneself cultivate the attention and sensitivity needed to gain insight into the truth of all phenomena. If one is stagnated by the joy of meditative absorption, one will lose the opportunity to advance and develop insightful realization of truth.

To return to our discussion of dhyana (meditative absorption), one might wonder why the fourth absorption is more remarkable than the joyful state in the third. It turns out that the meditative attainment at this stage can move one beyond the state of serenity and make one's mind clear. To provide an example, it is like someone learning about the world when their vision is limited by glasses of a certain color or thickness— what they see will be tainted by distortion. The attainment of the fourth absorption is like taking off those colored or thick glasses, and then the world is at last presented in a truthful way. When one reaches the fourth absorption, the level of concentration and sensitivity is paramount; one can have insight into the truth of all phenomena and break free from the prison of self-love.

SINGER: Is this state of enlightenment a state in which one continues to live without attachment, and is it therefore a joyful state again?

CHAO-HWEI: Yes. It can be called the joy of dharma. At this moment, the practitioner is still alive; their physiological functions are normal because the body has not decayed. But at this stage they will not be disturbed by the possibility of death. According to a microscopic observation of their own body, they know it is formed from a pile of molecules combined together and then disintegrating, rather than believing the illusion of solidity with which the body is normally mistaken. This experience will make the practitioner completely give up love and attachment toward themself. For example, if we watch TV and see very handsome and beautiful stars in a touching storyline, we invest pleasant feelings in that lasting image on the screen and are attracted by the plot. But if we fast-forward, we realize that the images are composed of many flickering frames, and we will not feel good about these constantly changing or flickering images. At this moment, if we turn off the TV, we may feel relieved because these disturbing images finally disappear.

If we realize that our bodies are like the gathering foam and our hearts are like water bubbles, when we face our own death, it is like seeing a leaf falling from a tree. There is neither an unwillingness to let go nor a strong desire to move on to the next journey; this is so-called nirvana.

SINGER: For somebody who is still in the midst of attachment to life, as I am, this is a difficult idea to grasp.

CHAO-HWEI: That's true. That is why the Buddha teaches people how to attain physical and mental happiness rather than how to reach nirvana.

SINGER: You have referred to the next life. That idea was present in the story of the young Brahmin who asked the Buddha how he could promote his happiness in the next life. You also said that if I share resources to benefit others now, I would have more joy in a future life. What is the basis in Buddhism for the belief that there is a next life?

CHAO-HWEI: In fact, the Buddha was not eager to prove whether there is a future life or not. He was most concerned with how to attain happiness in this present life, and that is also the very thing that concerns you the most. Most of his teachings focus on how humankind can attain happiness in this present life. As for your or my karma from our actions, if karma really does generate results, the consequences will ripen in our future lives, but we will not see them in the present moment. Even if the Buddha can see how karma works and tells us what he sees, he does not care whether we believe him or not. Just like the state of nirvana, it is futile to describe it to someone who has never experienced it. It does not matter how hard you try to make someone understand, if their meditative experience is not deep enough, they will not have the actual experience of nirvana. The Buddha's teachings are mainly based on the foundation of the common experience between the teacher and the students.

Hence there are two possible approaches: One is that the Buddha encourages those who can go deeper into their experiences and expand their range of awareness so they may personally experience the deeper truth of all phenomena. The other is that if a person is not willing to seek deeper truth by experiencing the necessary stages, then we simply respect their decision. Regardless, everyone has to live up to, or pay for, the consequences of the choices made in their lives. The Buddha merely spoke from his experience as an enlightened being and truthfully shared his discoveries of perceiving the truth of all phenomena. He tried his best to reveal that if you follow his teachings, establish correct understanding, and apply the correct way to practice meditation, at some point you will also experience what he experienced and prove his words true. This will happen naturally when one's practice matures without necessarily having to wait until future lives. Here is an example to clarify. The Buddha sees there is a cliff up ahead, but we cannot see it. Out of compassion, the Buddha would warn us, "Hey, there is a cliff. Watch out!" However, whether we keep going or not is our decision. We can choose to move forward or believe the Buddha and immediately stop.

SINGER: Very good. This brings me to another point I'd like to discuss. If we are focused on this life—let's say that it is somebody like me who is skeptical that there is another life— there has, ever since the dawn of Western philosophy in ancient Greece, been a problem about how we overcome the apparent conflict between morality and self-interest. Sometimes they will coincide, but sometimes what we ought to do will be one thing, and what it is in our best interest to do will be something quite different. According to Immanuel Kant, this conflict takes the form of a conflict between reason and our desires. Henry Sidgwick, the great nineteenth-century English utilitarian philosopher, holds that there are two different kinds of rational intuition: one tells us to "take the point of view of the universe" and recognize that the interests of everyone else count as much as ours; the other says that we have a special reason to be more concerned about our own interests than the interests of anyone else. Sidgwick was baffled by the contradiction between these two rational insights and felt that his failure to reconcile them showed that our conduct could not be put on a completely rational basis.[1]

Christians can resolve this problem by appealing to an afterlife in which we are rewarded in heaven if we act ethically and are punished in hell if we sin. What does Buddhism say here? Can Buddhism overcome this conflict between ethics and self-interest, without appeal to a life after the death of the body?

CHAO-HWEI: Allow me to verify whether I understood your question or not. Are you trying to inquire about the ethics regarding altruism versus self-benefiting? You accept the perspective of altruism, don't you?

SINGER: I do believe that morality should be concerned with benefiting others, but the question I am asking now is slightly different. Sidgwick did think of it as a question within ethics because he treated egoism—that is, the idea that we always ought to pursue our own interests—as a view within the sphere of ethics. Other philosophers see egoism as an external rival to ethics and therefore regard the conflict to which I am referring as a conflict between ethics and an alternative view that is concerned only with self-interest and not troubled about what is the right thing to do. Then the question is, how do we respond to the person who simply says, "I just care about myself and my family and some close friends. I don't care about others. If, for example, people are starving because of a drought in Africa, I don't care about that, and I am not going to do anything to help them."

How to respond to such a person is a problem in Western philosophy. It goes back at least to Plato's *Republic* in which Socrates is challenged by Glaucon to show that it is rational to act ethically, even when it seems that we can benefit by doing what is wrong. To support his case, Glaucon refers to the story of the ring of Gyges. According to an ancient Greek legend, Gyges was a shepherd who found a ring that made him invisible. He used the ring to kill the king and make himself king instead. Glaucon asks Socrates to show that what Gyges did was not only wrong but also contrary to reason. Now we find ourselves, twenty-five hundred years later, with the same question: What do we say to people whose attitude to others in need is "I just don't care about them; they have nothing to do with me"? How would you respond to that question from a Buddhist perspective?

CHAO-HWEI: This question guides us to the third stage of the Buddha's teaching, which is called the Path of the Bodhisattva. Bodhisattva acts are equal to altruism. Please allow me to offer a brief review of the three stages of the Buddha's teaching.

The first stage teaches people how to attain happiness in the present or in future lives. The second stage teaches people how to stop the cycle between birth and death and attain nirvana. This path is commonly referred to as the Path of Liberation. Those who pursue the second stage understand that the problem of suffering is rooted in self-love and the attachment to and cherishing of the illusion of the body and mind, which comes from ignorance (the inability to have insight into the truth of phenomena). As a result, to eliminate suffering completely means to solve the problem generated from self-love; other actions will not alleviate this problem. Based on the principle of compassion, these practitioners cannot bear to hurt other beings. Nevertheless, their mission is to focus on letting go of self-attachment to attain enlightenment. The Buddha's teachings, however, did not stop there.

The third level, the stage of selflessness and altruism, is commonly referred to as the Bodhisattva Path. The Buddha encouraged us to become bodhisattvas and not to limit ourselves with self-concern. At this level, self-love turns around and becomes a nourishing source of altruism. Practicing bodhisattva actions helps practitioners gain a clear insight into other people's circumstances and develop compassion—knowing that other people are just like them. Because of self-love, we all want to stay alive and fear death; we all pursue happiness and avoid suffering. Therefore, practitioners should share their resources in an active way, from a pure and selfless place of wanting to eliminate the suffering of others and take care of others' needs. We are willing to endure physical exhaustion and even pain in order to let other people remain free from suffering and attain happiness. In contrast, the practitioners who choose the Path of Liberation stay away from communities and villages to avoid disturbances to their meditation practice and therefore have few opportunities to participate in such altruistic acts.

When someone is able to shift from self-love to expand their ability to feel for and understand others, they will develop the capacity for feeling pain and enjoying comfort. In the same way, all other beings must have feelings and needs similar to ours. Eventually bodhisattva practitioners will be able to extend that kindness into more difficult situations. If they can increasingly treat more beings like that, it eventually becomes a habit. In the long run, bodhisattva practitioners will keep this quality of altruism in future lives and even enjoy themselves in the process of helping others. In Chinese, we call this life habit or altruistic tendency to help others "having the heart of a bodhisattva."

The altruistic tendencies and habitual patterns that have been cultivated through several lifetimes are as deeply rooted as instincts. Such people do not have concern about themselves; they only take delight in helping others. With this continual practice, because their interest is focused on serving others, their self-love and attachment diminish. In contrast to the second group (the Path of Liberation) of practitioners who focus very much on themselves and are dedicated to seeking ways to go beyond self-attachment, bodhisattva practitioners are accustomed to being considerate of others, and this habit makes them less and less self-centered—naturally they have fewer afflictions. According to the Buddhist scriptures, before the Buddha reached enlightenment, he might have been an elephant, a macaque, a moose, a dolphin, or a whale. But even if he were previously incarnated in the animal realm, he always possessed that altruistic quality and could easily sacrifice himself for his group. This altruistic attitude and its resulting actions across species still seem to hold on to self-attachment, but potentially, the self-attachment gradually dissolves during the process. Bodhisattvas possess boundless compassion and are beyond the binary opposition of sex, hierarchy, ethnicity, and species and therefore are called the "immeasurable samadhi." *Samadhi* means "concentration." The immeasurable samadhi means one's mind is concentrated on compassionate actions. This state of mind is immense and has no boundaries between self and others; hence, it is called immeasurable. When one reaches such a boundless and selfless state, the issue of self-attachment naturally fades away.

This is precisely why in the scriptures of the Mahayana tradition, the Buddha hoped that all beings could one day enter the third stage. Nonetheless, if people wished to accomplish the first stage, he taught them methods of pursuing happiness at the first stage. If someone wished to go to the second stage, he taught them to attain liberation in the second stage. However, the Buddha praised the third stage the most. In the third stage, the perfected practice is called *anuttara-samyak-sambodhi*, which means "supreme perfect enlightenment." No state of perfect awareness surpasses this; hence, it is called supreme. We Buddhists do not say we believe in the Buddha as in the kind of belief one has for God. We are emulating the Buddha and hope to learn to live like a bodhisattva acts and take more altruistic actions.

SINGER: I wonder if you would be prepared to comment on a view I hold about what we ought to do when we can help others in great need without sacrificing anything of comparable importance. I first put this view forward more than forty years ago in an essay called "Famine, Affluence and Morality," and I have restated it in my book *The Life You Can Save*. I ask readers to imagine that they are walking past a shallow pond when they see that a small child has fallen into the water and is in danger of drowning. What would you do? Perhaps the first reaction would be to look for an adult, perhaps a parent, who is caring for the child, but it seems that no one else is there. Your next thought would be to wade into the pond and rescue the child. You can easily do this, because you know that the pond is not deep, but you will get wet and muddy, and you will ruin your clothes and your shoes, which are expensive ones that you have just bought. Saving the child therefore comes at some cost to yourself. Nevertheless, almost everyone says that they would rescue the child and that to let the child drown because you did not want to ruin your expensive shoes would be seriously wrong.

I then point out that according to the United Nations Children's Fund (UNICEF), five million children died last year, most of them from preventable, poverty-related causes. Anyone who has some money to spare can help to prevent some of those deaths by contributing to, for example, the Against Malaria Foundation. This is a highly effective charity that distributes mosquito nets in malaria-prone regions to protect against malaria, a major killer of young children. If we think it would be wrong not to save the child drowning in the pond at the cost of ruining our expensive shoes, we should also think it is wrong not to donate to organizations that are saving the lives of children living in extreme poverty in developing countries. The fact that we cannot see the child or identify which child we will be saving is not ethically relevant. Each child saved is just as much a real child, with parents who will grieve over the child's death, as the child in the pond.

Now I come to the point that is relevant to the discussion we have been having. In "Famine, Affluence and Morality," I didn't write about what might motivate people, not only to help the drowning child in front of them, where there is a direct emotional bond because they can see the child, but also to help the child in a distant country, for whom there is no emotional connection. You have described the compassionate helping acts of the bodhisattva, which are based on both instinct and habit, developed by practice. Is that how Buddhist teachings solve this problem of helping distant strangers to whom one has no emotional connection?

CHAO-HWEI: For common people, the ability to be empathetic to strangers in a distant land can indeed not compare with seeing them in person. As a result, when one practices the immeasurable samadhi and visualizes extending one's loving-kindness, one is normally taught to do so from near to far and from close relationships to distant ones. In modern times, our feelings of strangeness and alienation toward these foreign strangers can be resolved by other people's descriptions of their circumstances or by shared media like videos.

When facing a drowning child, a strong compassion suddenly arises, pushing us to actively try to help. The working of the mind will actually extend our own self-love because we try to help an unknown drowning child. Normally, we have emotional connections with our family, friends, and community, but if we expand our compassion in this way, eventually there will be a limit on how far we will go; thus, it cannot be called immeasurable. In this process we have an extension of the self to the others we love. This is self-love with a larger boundary. This attitude divides all things into two categories: either they belong to me, or I belong to them. The extension derived from these two inner attitudes is self-centered.

There is a Chinese ideal that one should sacrifice individual welfare for the greater good, but this is not the Buddhist altruistic attitude. The Chinese altruistic ideal will eventually hit a boundary. No matter how large the space enclosed by the boundary is, there is still a boundary. It is therefore always possible that the person who claims to sacrifice their individual welfare for the greater good also has to sacrifice anyone who is outside the boundary of the greater good they define, such as people of other ethnicities, or animals. In this manner, someone who is a hero for one group—perhaps a particular nation or race—can turn out to be a villain for another. It's extremely difficult for such a person to be aware of this mistake because they are filled with the honor of being a hero. They will be praised and admired by people, so their faults might not be condemned compared to those of more selfish people. Because of this, the "hero" might even have less chance of reflection. From the Buddhist perspective, this way of thinking does not transcend the self (ego); it just expands its territory, and if it begins with self-interest, then it is not truly altruistic.

However, the practice of immeasurable samadhi (the boundless state) is different. As already mentioned, rather than expanding one's own territory, the boundless state is about dissolving one's self (ego) through the process of exchanging self for other. That is the difference between compassion and love for the greater good. A bodhisattva does not love the drowning child due to a certain connection; instead, they turn the limited love (that we typically only have toward ourselves or those close to us) into a strong concern for this child's well-being. The point of "limitless qualities" is not about extending the boundaries of self, but rather the dissolution of the boundary between self and others. The mechanism of altruism, regardless of whether it is one to one or one to many, can eliminate the boundary between oneself and others. In these different ways, compassion, self-love, and the love we only extend to those close to us determines the great difference between a limited state and a boundless state of mind.

SINGER: If we say to somebody who is still within the limited mind, "You ought to help strangers," they will see that as something they don't want to do. We are asking them to sacrifice things that they enjoy, such as spending money on themselves and their families. If I understood what you said, you are agreeing that at first this will be perceived as a sacrifice, but when one is in the third stage and constantly practices bodhisattva acts of helping others and this becomes a habit, then what was first perceived as a sacrifice instead becomes a delight. Have I understood that correctly?

CHAO-HWEI: Yes, it is a source of delight.

SINGER: So it's a matter of somehow making a start with acts of helping others and then practicing and developing the habit of doing so?

CHAO-HWEI: Yes, but I want to emphasize that bodhisattva practitioners do not help others because they want to take delight in such acts. The more bodhisattva practitioners focus on helping others, the less self-centered their state of mind becomes. They will start naturally and will eventually receive the joy of selflessness. That joy is immense, and it comes without the bodhisattva practitioner striving for it.

Now I would like to return to your earlier question, which was, how do we persuade people to act altruistically toward strangers, including distant strangers with whom they have no emotional connection? Augustine, one of the major thinkers of the early Christian Church (354–430 C.E.) considered self-centered love and strong desire to be burdens called sin, with human beings being incapable of helping themselves out of sin and instead having to rely on the grace of God. Thomas Aquinas, as we saw earlier, proposed four cardinal virtues according to the rationality of humans: a sense of justice, courage, the wisdom to tell right from wrong, and self-control. Nevertheless, he argued if you do not believe in God, you will not have the three supernatural virtues of faith, hope, and charity. According to Christian teachings, if you want to love others, including less connected neighbors, total strangers, or even enemies against whom you have negative emotions, you need to seek the source of love in God. Only then will you be able to love others. So Christians will likely answer your question this way: you first begin by loving God, and then you will be able to love others. This logic makes God seem like the source of electricity. One charges one's batteries through one's connection with him, and only then will one be able to do good.

Buddhism takes an entirely different view. From the Buddhist perspective, the source of altruism comes from the capacity to feel another's pain. With this ability, we are able to break the barrier between self and others and generate a feeling of empathetic consciousness—called compassion in Buddhism

KEY BUDDHIST CONCEPTS: KARMA AND NIRVANA | 51

and conscience in Confucianism—that does not derive from an external source like the grace of God. As long as we are willing to cultivate it, this quality can be developed from inside. We are all capable of expanding our compassion. It turns out that no individual is closed or isolated from the outer world. Our sensations and intentions are connected with other lives through obvious or hidden channels, and through these channels, we are able to perceive others' pain and suffering. On the surface, when we witness suffering or hear the wails of other sentient beings, empathetic compassion arises. On a more hidden and subtle level, even if we don't see their painful expressions or hear their cries, we are still able to perceive these strong emotions.

Nonetheless, to ordinary people, this kind of capability is limited to those they are close to. A mother's love, for example, is demonstrated in her care of her children. She seems to be capable of sensing whether her child is healthy or happy, even when her child is not in her presence. When her child is in intense pain or experiences a major disaster, a mother sometimes feels an inexplicable uneasiness or sorrow. Thus, for ordinary people, this powerful sensation can pierce through the barrier between self and others, though it is normally limited to our own family members with whom we share a deep connection, while we remain indifferent to what happens to strangers.

However, when we transform from ordinary to extraordinary beings like selfless, altruistic bodhisattvas who have reached the state of nonself and experience no self-other barrier, we are able to feel the sufferings of all beings as a mother would her child's. When we develop ourselves from ordinary people to enlightened beings like bodhisattvas, we are able to gradually cultivate and expand our perception and compassion toward others' pain through our intention and action. As long as we are still in this world of dependent origination, our lives are not isolated. There are many ways to build deeper connections with others if we do not intentionally sever our connection with other people's lives. We may even be able to transcend and transform these connections into compassion.

SINGER: Can you tell me how, on a practical level, we can break down the barriers people have between the self and others?

CHAO-HWEI: Here I would like to use the example of a local Taiwanese charity organization, Tzu Chi Foundation, whose care extends to strangers in other countries. During your previous visit to Taiwan, we traveled to Hualien on the east coast of Taiwan. There we visited the Tzu Chi nunnery, where this organization started, and had lunch with the founding Venerable Master Cheng Yen. Perhaps you remember the story of how, in 1966, she learned that an indigenous woman had an obstructed labor and had been carried by her family from her tribal village in the mountains to a clinic in a small town in Hualien to seek medical help. The whole process took eight hours. Nevertheless, she was turned away because the family could not afford the advance payment required. Master Cheng Yen felt empathetic to this situation, which inspired her to invite thirty local followers to donate five cents per day to establish an organization to relieve suffering for those in desperate need of help; this organization became Tzu Chi. Her initial intention was to build a hospital in Hualien that did not charge advance payment in hopes that no one would ever again be denied medical help due to poverty. Well, you know what happened, because you saw the large modern Tzu Chi General Hospital and the adjacent Tzu Chi University, which is renowned for the quality of its School of Medicine. Tzu Chi Foundation is now an international organization, ten million members strong, many of them active volunteers, with chapters in forty-seven countries.

Venerable Cheng Yen has been breaking down the barriers between self and others in a very practical way for the past fifty years and has been extremely successful in doing so. Her answer to your question of how to do that was, "Just do it." Perhaps in the beginning, those thirty followers just responded to the request of this venerable and may even have had to convince themselves to participate. However, one will discover from doing the work of helping others that the venerable's words are wise: "Just do it." After initially having to force ourselves to enjoy helping others, helping others becomes a habit that just naturally happens. If we continue straight on this path, eventually we find that even if we are busy with altruistic work and have limited time for meditation, the barrier between self and others still gradually dissolves, and we will still reach liberation. This is what is referred to as the inconceivable state of liberation in the scriptures of Mahayana.

SINGER: Thank you. I do remember that inspiring visit to Hualien, to the hospital, and of course to the monastery and meeting with Venerable Cheng Yen. What she has achieved is a very illuminating example of Buddhism in practice, and it leads me to the next question I have, especially as you mentioned Tzu Chi. It is often said in the West that whereas Christianity looks outward to help others and encourages good works, especially helping the poor, Buddhism is more inward-looking. You yourself said earlier that meditators look inward to achieve enlightenment. I already noticed during my previous visit that you, Venerable, seem to have a different view. Like Venerable Cheng Yen, you have founded an organization, the Life Conservation Association (LCA), to protect animals in Taiwan, and LCA now has a hundred members, a few hundred sponsors and volunteers, and has garnered many important achievements in the field of animal protection. Is the idea that Buddhism is inward-looking just a myth that is common in the West? Or is there something different about Buddhism in Taiwan that has allowed you and Venerable Cheng Yen to be more involved with the world?

CHAO-HWEI: Rather than saying that the Tzu Chi Foundation and LCA prompted Buddhism, which values inner reflection, to develop an outward-reaching style to help the world, I would say that both paths have always coexisted. This is not an overnight change. Among Buddhists, some put more emphasis on meditation, while others put it on altruism. Today, there is an organization, the International Network of Engaged Buddhists (INEB), that gathers many engaged Buddhists from different parts of the world who either lead or proactively participate in various altruistic projects.

However, it is undeniable that the development of Buddhism in Taiwan catches the attention of the Buddhist communities around the world. The founder and president of INEB, Ajarn Sulak, is impressed with the contributions that Taiwanese Buddhist groups have made to society, and I can list two major developments here. First, although the land of Taiwan is small, it gathers and garners powerful Buddhist energy and is the home of three enormously devoted Buddhist communities (Buddha's Light Mountain, Tzu Chi, and Dharma Drum Mountain) that propagate the concept of "Buddhism for the World" and promote the spirit of engaged Buddhism—in other words, Buddhism in service to the world. With the support of their followers, these communities are able to perform charitable acts based on effective altruism on a global scale. Second, many female monastics (also referred to as *bhikkhunis*) frequently form independent sanghas (spiritual communities) and are widely trusted in our society. Their communities demonstrate outstanding capabilities, have ample resources, and provide outstanding care for our society. So far, these two characteristics are what distinguish Taiwanese Buddhist communities and make them shining examples to the rest of the world.

SINGER: I met the founder and some members of the International Network of Engaged Buddhists at the conference on animal welfare that I attended here in Taiwan two years ago.

CHAO-HWEI: That's right. I remember we had dinner with Mr. Lokamitra, who is from England but has been working in India for a long time to assist the Dalit caste and promote Buddhism to more people. His father was a renowned anthropologist, and Mr. Lokamitra studied Buddhism from the time he was young. He later created Nagaloka Center in Nagpur, India, and also established Nargarjuna Training Institute to help the so-called untouchables or Dalits. He himself is a member of INEB. Mr. Lokamitra advocates globally for Dr. Bhimrao Ambedkar's ideas. Dr. Ambedkar was independent India's first minister of law and justice and led four hundred thousand people to take refuge in Buddhism. With the fundamental idea of Buddhism that all beings are equal, he campaigned against social discrimination against the untouchables and women. Both Dr. Ambedkar and Mr. Lokamitra are exemplary figures of altruism in the Buddhist world.

SINGER: Thank you. I am pleased to learn that there are many engaged Buddhists, and not only in Taiwan. But now I'm wondering whether, in your view, some people might spend too much time in meditation. In asking this question, I am of course aware that here we are guests in a center for meditation, and I do not wish to be disrespectful in any way. My question arises, however, from a discussion I had with Matthieu Ricard. I am not sure if you know him or have heard of him. He's a French Buddhist who is an assistant to the Dalai Lama, and he lives in Nepal for part of each year. He became quite famous in the West because he took part in a study of the brains of people who meditate, and scientists observed that when he was meditating on compassion, his brain produced a level of gamma waves that they had never seen before. Gamma waves are associated with attention, consciousness, and learning. The scientists also reported that he had an unusual amount of activity in his brain's left prefrontal cortex when compared with the right counterpart. This supposedly showed that he has a much larger capacity for happiness than most people, and this earned him the nickname of "the happiest man in the world."

He himself regards this as just media exaggeration. I met him in Paris not long ago when we were both speakers at an event to rally support for animal protection and not eating meat, and then he came to Princeton to talk about altruism, a subject on which he has written a big book.[2] In that book he mentions people who have spent twenty, thirty, and even forty thousand hours in meditation. If someone were to spend eight hours a day, seven days a week, meditating, it would still take them more than thirteen years to meditate for forty thousand hours. So I wonder whether, from the perspective of people in the third group you mentioned—that is, practitioners of bodhisattva acts—it is possible to meditate too much. Should people who meditate so much be spending less time on meditation and more time on social activism?

CHAO-HWEI: Your question has touched on an ongoing tension that has existed in the Buddhist world for a long time. People who practice the Path of the Bodhisattva are inclined to engage in the world and perform altruistic acts due to their nature. Their lives are so full with altruistic work that they cannot spend too much time on meditation. The practitioners on the Liberation Path will then say to them, "You are not paying attention to the core of all problems. The key is to eliminate self-love and afflictions. What you are doing are things outside the core." The Buddha guided these two kinds of practitioners with two separate approaches so they both gain maximum benefit. For those who focus on eliminating self-attachment and attaining nirvana, the Buddha offered the teaching of the Path of Liberation. When these practitioners walk that path, they eventually attain the state of arhat, which is highly acclaimed. At least these people have moved beyond their ego and no longer cause problems by hurting others.

SINGER: That's true.

CHAO-HWEI: The reason I call this a constant tension is because we are talking about two different forms of Buddhism—Hinayana and Mahayana. The former is a term that only appeared in traditional Mahayana Buddhist texts referring to non-Mahayana texts and practitioners. The word *Hinayana* literally means "lesser vehicle," which is a metaphor referring to practitioners on the path who focus on personal liberation. In contrast, *Mahayana* (great vehicle) practitioners want not only to attain enlightenment for themselves but also for the sake of all others. These two schools are like two different types of vehicles; one carries more passengers whereas the other, just one. The latter school refers to themselves as Theravadan practitioners and refuses to be called Hinayana.

SINGER: When you say, of those who focus on their own enlightenment, "at least they will not be hurting others," that's true and it's good, but is it enough? I use the example of the drowning child precisely to make the point that not hurting others is not enough. If I see the drowning child in the pond and I don't save the child so they drown, I can still say, "I did not hurt the child." There is a sense in which that claim is true. I didn't push the child into the pond. If I had not been anywhere near the pond, the child would still have drowned. But on my view, that's not good enough. If you could have saved the child, at a minor cost to yourself, and you did not, you have done something wrong. Similarly, to say that people who are spending large amounts of time in meditation are not hurting others is not sufficient grounds for saying that they are living a fully ethical life.

CHAO-HWEI: I agree with you, and this is why the Mahayana thinks Theravada should cultivate more altruistic capacity and behavior. To be frank, some Buddhists don't see eye to eye due to their respective choice of path, but some are able to accept the choice of others and acknowledge their value.

SINGER: Then if I were a Buddhist, I would be a Mahayana Buddhist! I am glad that we agree on that. And I think this would be a good place to stop and have lunch.

CHAPTER 3

Women and Equality

SINGER: That was a splendid lunch, and I was delighted to see that no animals were harmed for it. I was also pleased to meet the other monastics living here. This beautiful place is, if I understand correctly, run by women for women. Chao-Hwei, you have a reputation for being a feminist. I have heard that you once tore up, in public, the Buddhist rules that make female Buddhist monastics subordinate to monks. Is that right?

CHAO-HWEI: It is.

SINGER: I greatly admire that gesture, and I would like to know more about the thinking behind it. The religions I am most familiar with are strongly patriarchal. How does your feminism fit within Buddhist thought?

CHAO-HWEI: Buddhist communities lack the centralized control that you would be familiar with from examples like the Roman Catholic Church, where all decisions flow down from the top of the power structure. Even so, Buddhist female aspirants face exposure to authoritative Buddhist scriptures that suggest and often convince the reader that women are subordinate to men. Despite the absence of centralized control, many women willingly subordinate themselves to men. A single social movement alone cannot bring about great changes here. For this reason, I am making a constant effort to deconstruct the authority of the so-called sacred scriptures.

Fortunately, this attitude of "audacious skepticism toward sacred authority" is rooted in the Buddha's teachings. The four *agamas*, known as the five *nikayas* in Pali in the Theravada[1] tradition, are the most important early Buddhist texts. The collection of texts includes the well-known Kalama Sutta (AN 3.65). In this sutra, the Kalamas of Kesaputta say to the Buddha, "Lord, there are some priests and contemplatives who come to Kesaputta. They expound and glorify their own doctrines, but as for the doctrines of others, they deprecate them, revile them, show contempt for them, and disparage them. Then other priests and contemplatives come to Kesaputta. They expound and glorify their own doctrines, but as for the doctrines of others, they deprecate them, revile them, show contempt for them, and disparage them. They leave us absolutely uncertain and in doubt. Which of these venerable priests and contemplatives are speaking the truth, and which ones are lying?"

The Buddha's answer is, "Of course you are uncertain, Kalamas. Of course you are in doubt. When there are reasons for doubt, uncertainty is born. In this case, Kalamas, don't go by reports, by legends, by traditions, by scripture, by logical conjecture, by inference, by analogies, by agreement through pondering views, by probability, or by the thought 'This contemplative is our teacher.' When you know for yourselves that 'these qualities are unskillful; these qualities are blameworthy; these qualities are criticized by the wise; these qualities, when adopted and carried out, lead to harm and to suffering,' then you should abandon them."[2]

The Kalama Sutta provides a set of references that helps one examine the truth of the doctrines. Rather than embracing the words of authority, one should trust empirical evidence. We should always ask ourselves, "Does this doctrine lead us closer to happiness and alleviate suffering?" In terms of ethics, we may ask, "Does this doctrine inspire people to be kind?" These principles are helpful when I am approaching the narration of these canonical works with critical thinking in order to create a solid conclusion. I believe the sexist content should be removed from the Buddhist canon.

There is another historical factor worthy of consideration. The Buddha's words were not written the moment he taught. The commonly referenced canonical works were remembered, collected, and written down after his passing. So it is helpful to keep in mind that it was only after the Buddha's death that the *bhikkhus* (also referred to as male monastics or Buddhist monks) collected and compiled his teachings. Long story short, the power of compiling and interpreting canonical works belongs to male monastics. These Indian bhikkhus are raised in a cultural background with deep-rooted gender biases. Could some prejudice have slipped into the texts in the name of "the Buddha's words"? I have enough reasons to remain carefully skeptical.

I'll give an example. There is a passage that says a monk can speak about the wrongdoings of female monastics, but female monastics cannot speak about the wrongdoings of the monks. Right away I can find a contradictory passage in a record from the Buddha's time. The Vinaya is the Buddhist classic that records the rules of the sangha and the reasons why Buddha formulated such regulations, in addition to the methodology for judging the severity of crimes and various other precedents. Established after the formation of the male sangha, the

community of female monastics lacked experience in forming
a sangha and lived a practical spiritual life. At the beginning
of the bhikkhuni sangha's establishment, the Buddha told the
bhikkhu sangha to send some male precept holders to fulfill the
obligation of educating the new female members in the way of
the sangha, rather than point out their faults. At one point, a
group of monks, now known as the Six Monks,[3] was involved
in the observation of the female monastics' sangha. Throughout the process, they failed to adhere to proper behavior. For
example, once when the Six Monks lectured female monastics,
instead of discussing important topics with them—such as
monastic vows, meditation, wisdom, and views on liberation
and nonattachment—they talked about conflicts, women, lust,
and gourmet food, and even mimicked the sounds of peacocks
and cranes. They danced around and pretended to walk with
a limp. As a result, Buddha's aunt, Prajapati, herself a female
monastic, went to the Buddha and reported the Six Monks'
improper behavior. According to the record, the Buddha did
not say to her, "Oh, you are a female monastic; you may not
speak ill of the monks." In fact, the record shows that he instead
summoned the monks to investigate the truth of the reported
misdeeds. According to the Vinaya, the Buddha chastised the
Six Monks, saying, "Your behavior is utterly inappropriate.
Not only do you lack dignified manners, but you also don't act
like Buddhist practitioners. Your speech is improper, and your
conduct has deviated from the right track. How can you guide
the female monastics when your own integrity is sullied?" He
not only berated the Six Monks but told all the monks, "From
now on, it is not your place to appoint yourselves as their
guides. Instead, we will have a sangha meeting, and we will
send the monks whom our sangha unanimously considers to
be qualified to guide them."[4]

We can use this case as a counterargument to the rule that monks may talk about the wrongdoings of female monastics, but female monastics may not speak ill of monks. The details of the Vinaya provide ample reasons to suspect that bhikkhus had been overextending their authority to control the behavior of bhikkhunis. Another example of monks abusing their power can be observed in their interaction with laypeople. In the Vinaya, the Buddha clearly stipulates that trusted laypersons can report the faults of the monks to the sangha.[5] However, the present climate of the Buddhist tradition witnesses the shunning of regulation by monks who turn a blind eye to possible criticism from trusted laypeople.[6] Time and time again, such monks assert that laypeople have no right to interfere in monks' behavior.

So I located all the contradictory passages in the scriptures and refuted them one by one to show all the flaws and fallacies that gave ample reasons to overrule the contradictions. And what was the outcome? Although some monastics had true admiration for what I did, and supported it, others sought to downplay the effect of my dissent. Some monks, both male and female, continued doing what had always been done—ignoring the necessity to overturn the rule subordinating female monastics to male monks. If we did engage as a monastic community in the discussion over this inequality, some monks would insist on a hushed environment, saying, "We should not air our dirty laundry in public."

But I don't believe that we should keep these problems within our community—otherwise, Buddhists will never make progress. Even though discrimination between men and women still exists in the secular world, general circumstances are still more progressive than within the monastic community. I felt that I needed to expose the sexism in the monastic tradition to the public, so people would ask, "Wow, is this really what's going on in the Buddhist community? Are you really going through all these difficulties?" I thought that such a public reaction could create pressure that might accelerate the pace of change within the monastic community. The key was to find the proper occasion to expose the sexist rules to the public. Understanding how to confront such huge, everlasting structures of sexist practices was an incredibly challenging task with such limited resources.

Then His Holiness the Dalai Lama was scheduled to visit Taiwan in the spring of 2001, which provided us with a focal point and opportunity to expose the sexist rules in the Buddhist community to the public. He was going to talk about "new moral thinking in the twenty-first century" according to the announcement from the organization that brought him to Taiwan. I made a public announcement to the Dalai Lama and told him, "Moral thinking in the new century happens to correspond to the Buddhist concept of equality for all beings, which fundamentally challenges the moral perspectives of male chauvinists and human chauvinists. Taiwanese Buddhist communities demonstrate advanced progress in the above issues. Therefore, I would like to invite His Holiness to consider learning from our development while propagating dharma teachings in Taiwan." I made it truly clear to the Dalai Lama that even though monks and female monastics belong to two separate spiritual communities in Taiwan, sexual discrimination still exists. The women in Tibetan Buddhism have an even worse situation; in the Tibetan tradition, communities of female monastics are not even allowed to exist.

Nevertheless, we believe the Dalai Lama maintains an open mind toward the reinstitution of female monastics in the Tibetan tradition. Two female Australian monks, who had been ordained as novices by the Dalai Lama, later received full ordination as female monastics in Taiwan. Even so, they are not accepted within the Tibetan tradition. Even today, His Holiness fails to allow Tibetan women to receive full ordination as bhikkhunis. My intention was not to attack the Dalai Lama—I was trying to leverage this rare opportunity to emphasize a very important point and put the Buddhist community directly under pressure from public opinion. My attempt was to convey that even though David faced Goliath, he still stood a chance of winning.

The day before the arrival of the Dalai Lama in Taiwan, I held a press conference in Taipei City to make a public announcement to the Dalai Lama. I proclaimed that I would publicly tear up the *attha garudhamma* ("eight deferential practices")—a set of rules that created gender inequality in the Buddhist community—to demonstrate rejection of the precepts subordinating female monastics to monks. The day the Dalai Lama came to Taiwan (March 31, 2001), there happened to be a large academic conference at the national academy of Taiwan, Academia Sinica. I made a speech at the opening ceremony of the conference, announcing the abolition of attha garudhamma. My unprecedented defiance to Buddhism received the same level of attention as His Holiness's arrival in Taiwan from the domestic media. Later, I learned from foreign friends that this act also attracted the attention of international media.

SINGER: What was the result of your courageous actions? Are female monastics here in Taiwan now equal with monks? Or are they still subject to control from men?

CHAO-HWEI: My actions did not, in themselves, end the system of bhikkhuni subordination; however, they have been most effective in raising awareness. My defiance created a shock wave and served as a real educational moment for the Buddhist community. Several female monastics came to me and shared their lived experiences of sexism. I had impressed them by staging a public rejection and disapproval of the authoritative doctrine with solid textual evidence. The female monastics were moved to tears of joy. Before, female monastics could only complain about and make objections to inequality in private, thinking, "Times have changed, circumstances have improved, so how can men still mistreat women like this?" Although they supported their appeal with modern thought, it lacked the authority of sacred texts. The monks would then reply, "But you should respect the words of the Buddha." The female monastics were silenced; at least until they saw me overthrow the authority of the so-called eight deferential practices in public with a thoughtful interpretation inspired by Buddhist canonical texts and careful logical reasoning. Then they were finally able to be freed from the conditioning of the sacred authority—the root source of this inequality.

SINGER: So the struggle for equality between the sexes is still continuing here in Taiwan and Buddhist communities in other countries as well?

CHAO-HWEI: I do not see this as a battle between the sexes. It is a battle between men and women who respect gender equality and men and women who disrespect gender equality. In the present system, both sexes are victims. Men, under the protection of the patriarchal mindset, become arrogant yet have an inferiority complex and have difficulty accepting the existence of outstanding bhikkhunis. At the same time, these monks lose opportunities to grow. I am not saying that all women are innocent either; they can be part of the conspiracy. Some bhikkhunis behave with extreme humility in front of the monks, and these acts create a certain inner imbalance. To compensate for the imbalance, these bhikkhunis act as if they are superior to laypeople. This shows that the bhikkhunis, too, are deep in the quagmire of the superiority complex (to overcome their feeling of inferiority to the male monks). Neither males nor females benefit from this situation. Their affliction does not decrease but increases, signifying a failure of their spiritual practice.

SINGER: You have written about this, haven't you?

CHAO-HWEI: I have published one book and several papers arguing that the issue of gender inequality has become so prevalent that it is like the air in our daily lives. Every day you can see men walking in front and women following, or maybe when seating arrangements are made at a meeting or ceremony, men sit in the front rows and women sit in the back. This is what I call the "gender order." These ubiquitous gender orders continue to reinforce gender discrimination in Buddhism. We have to engage in constant battles, because whenever such occasions arise, we must stage a very strong protest so as not to be regarded as acquiescing to the legitimacy of sex discrimination.

SINGER: I believe you also created a stir in Myanmar, the country of your birth. Please tell me what happened there.

CHAO-HWEI: Myanmar is a Buddhist country where women's status is far inferior to that of men. In Myanmar, there is a teacher named Venerable Pa-Auk (who is normally referred to as Pa-Auk Sayadaw). He is almost like an enlightened noble person (ariya-puggala) because he shows equal affection and compassion whether interacting with men or women. Our

Buddhist college Hong-Shi once invited Venerable Pa-Auk to teach a meditation course. I made it very clear that for the seating arrangement in the meditation hall, the monks should be on the left side, and the female monastics should be on the right. I would not allow the monks to be seated in front of the female monastics. From the photos we took, you can see that Venerable Pa-Auk was in the center with the men and women arranged equally on both sides.

When bhikkhunis and students at Hong-Shi Buddhist College welcomed Venerable Pa-Auk, his male followers walked right behind him, while the female followers walked farther behind, but I walked right next to him, refusing to conform to their gender order. Venerable Pa-Auk's response was to treat me just like a mischievous child. He was aware of these little psychological games.

When the Pa-Auk Forest Monastery had just been completed in Mawlamyine, in Myanmar, Venerable Pa-Auk invited me to join the opening ceremony, and I later visited the other Pa-Auk Meditation Center in Yangon with him. A chauvinistic bhikkhu from Taiwan posed as a mentor during this time and always gave Taiwanese bhikkhunis instructions. I immediately rebuked his behavior, which enraged him. He then grumbled to other Taiwanese lay male practitioners, saying, "When Chao-Hwei arrives for lunch tomorrow, I will make sure that she understands how insignificant female monastics are." According to the convention of Myanmar monasteries, when the bhikkhus and bhikkhunis line up for food, the older bhikkhus go first, followed by younger bhikkhus and male novices, then laymen. Only after all of them are served will it be the bhikkhunis, female novices, and laywomen's turn. (This is even worse than the traditional Buddhist order, in which monks go first, then female monastics, and laypeople behind them.) A kind layman overheard that bhikkhu's claim and informed me of what was about to occur.

I immediately met with Pa-Auk Sayadaw and complained directly to him. I said that the monk was acting like an emperor and always walked ahead of bhikkhunis. I had reprimanded him several times for his arrogant behavior, but he used the gender order Myanmar adheres to for food service in monasteries to belittle me. I then emphasized that in order to respect the Buddhist monastic order—male monks, female monastics, laymen, and laywomen—female monastics should not walk behind laymen. In fact, I do not believe even the bhikkhus are entitled to line up before bhikkhunis. Nevertheless, I did not take that radical stance out of the respect for local monastic culture. Rather, in order to establish the legitimacy of this request, I chose to reason with the meditation master based on the principle of "respect for precepts."

Then Sayadaw answered, "To encourage segregation of the sexes, we specifically avoid men and women walking among each other. If you pay attention, you will see that I, the Sayadaw, am always the last." I replied, "Master, the circumstance is completely different for you. Wherever you are, you are always on top, but we are not. If this order were insisted on for the sake of respecting the Buddha's regulations, I would stop eating." I persuaded the master, and he answered me with a bright smile, "Okay, I will change it immediately."

Next day, the master left early and returned to the Pa-Auk Forest Monastery in Mawlamyine to ensure an immediate adjustment was made in the queuing order for food service. At lunchtime, the female monastics and *sayalays* (devoted laywomen aspirants) no longer had to walk behind laymen. Many female monastics came to thank me for what I did, and some still do today. Since I made my objection, there has been a lasting change in queuing order to obtain food. Before that, even laymen looked down on the female monastics.

This is a very long answer to your original question about what happened after I staged the protest when the Dalai Lama came to visit. I can only tell you that gender inequality has been a common practice, and you can still see it everywhere.

SINGER: You have given me examples from Taiwan, Tibet, and Myanmar. Do you have others?

CHAO-HWEI: I do. Once I was invited to give a keynote speech at a huge international conference in Malaysia. A Malaysian Buddhist group undertook part of the preparations for the conference. The organizers invited participants to sit at tables outside the conference hall prior to the opening ceremonies in order to line up the participants in pairs before entering the conference hall to light candles dedicated to the Buddha statue. I heard the long list of names being called out in the order the organizer intended, but I had only heard a long list of bhikkhus' names. I thought, "Something must be wrong." So I questioned with a quiet voice, "Did you arrange all the monks before the female monastics?" The moderator quickly responded, "Wow, I hope this is not the case." He must have heard the severity of my voice and was somewhat daunted by that.

I waited patiently and finally heard my own name, and all the names following were those of the female monastics. I warned the organizers again that I could see the arrangement of all the male monks before the female monastics and that to protest this sexist gender order, I would refuse to partake in the opening ceremony. As the only keynote speaker invited to talk at that ceremony, I wanted to make the strongest possible objection to this gender order. Shocked by my reaction, the organizers immediately held an internal discussion to respond to my decision. Eventually the event staff arranged for the monks and the female monastics to walk in in two parallel lines. Even with the rearrangement of the procession, very few female monastics dared to walk next to the male monks. As a result, I was invited to walk at the front of the line, and the female monastics followed me.

I will never walk behind the male monks because that has a symbolic meaning, and I will not allow subordination of myself to the male monks in public. As a spiritual practitioner, it is a virtue of humility to walk behind one's companion. But as a Buddhist feminist activist, I must protest this kind of unreasonable gender order arrangement. On the other hand, I cannot always be a warrior; I cannot always take a fighting stance. I must find a balance. I will not shy away from such occasions, yet I also will not take the initiative to go to all the ceremonies where I could make public objections to what is happening to women. I do not consider myself the savior of women. Men alone did not create the situation of sexual discrimination that confronts women today; the cause is both males and females. It is fine for me to stage some sort of shocking educational experience, but beyond that it is up to other women to help themselves.

SINGER: Thank you for giving me this picture of what is happening with regard to gender inequality in Buddhism and of your own role in this narrative. Religions are often very slow to adapt to changes in thinking. The Roman Catholic Church still seems to be a very long way away from having a female Pope or even female priests. In some of the Protestant denominations, women are more equal, but generally gaining equality for women in religious institutions is hard work. And, of course, the same is true in other religions. So it's good to hear that you have been able to make some progress in Taiwan and are extending the struggle for equality to other Buddhist countries. Is there anything else you would like to add on this general issue of the position of women in religious institutions?

CHAO-HWEI: Thank you! Your attention, support, and encouragement really motivate me. I appreciate it from the bottom of my heart. To conclude our discussion, I do have a few more points I would like to add.

First, gender equality is valued in modern societies worldwide. However, Christianity, Islam, and Buddhism, which claim to be universal religions, are not necessarily advanced on this issue. Rather, their doctrines are usually obstacles to this kind of progress. Inspired and motivated by the zeitgeist of our times, some open-minded Christians have reflected on their tradition and developed feminist theology and queer theology to align its teachings with the movement of modern thought.

Second, what is it that holds religions back from acknowledging gender justice like their contemporary secular societies do? The answer might lie in the reverence religious insiders have for their sacred literature. Clergies or believers tend to regard sacred texts as "God's words" or "the Buddha's own words" and thus fortify the ultimate power these texts have. When unrealistic or unreasonable passages are discovered, they try their best to justify the contents. Anyone who dares to challenge the authority of holy scriptures will be regarded as a traitor attempting to demolish faith. It is rare to see an insider, like the Buddha in the Kalama Sutta, who is not afraid to deconstruct himself, subverting his own authority to train his followers to develop discerning wisdom, courage, and capacity. The Buddha's level of open-mindedness and graciousness is uncommon among religious insiders.

Third, given the fact that all major religions were born in ancient times, it is understandable that sexist comments would appear in sacred texts—using rules and behavioral protocols to restrict women and make sure they are only of secondary importance; quoting contents from sacred texts to define women's position (for example, bhikkhunis should walk behind bhikkhus); and suppressing women in every possible way (for instance, having laymen queuing in front of bhikkhunis). None of these phenomena are surprising to me.

I have always believed that "a ball placed on a slope will not remain in the same place"; it will 100 percent roll downhill. As long as the authority of these sacred texts remains unchallenged, then women's status will not stay in its initial place but will go downhill like the ball. This is precisely why, when I began to advocate for gender equality in the Buddhist community, not only did I leverage the zeitgeist as my major appeal to urge Buddhists to catch up with the progress of modern society, but I also went straight to the original source and challenged those sacred texts that made women inferior and positioned them on that downhill slope in the first place.

Fourth, the fact that gender inequality is more serious in religious communities than in general societies cannot be attributed to one single reason, such as the absolute submission to the authority of sacred literature. After long observation, I discovered that even in a strictly sexist environment, there could be exceptions, fortunate women who are cherished in their families. For example, daughters are deeply cherished by their fathers because of family ties, and wives are loved by their husbands due to their mutual bonding. These connections can somehow overturn women's inferior status.

As a result, after careful thought, I have concluded that in order to eliminate emotions that could pose difficulties for their spiritual practice, monks actively sever ties with their families or partners, which could potentially foster their bias against the opposite sex. To them, women are no longer dear daughters or beloved wives but a group of strangers. Spaces like Buddhist communities or Catholic congregations provide few or no opportunities for monks to interact with women. This may serve the purpose of spiritual purification, but the very same circumstance makes female practitioners lose not only the protection that originated from their family and partnership connection but also their individuality. They become a collective negative image that will potentially undermine the spiritual practice of male practitioners. This stigmatization makes them a target for male practitioners to avoid or suppress.

Fifth, the secular order is normally considered from multiple perspectives such as seniority, experience, contribution, and so on. It is impossible to determine the order based on one single aspect such as sexism. The sexism that ranks men as superior and women as inferior in the Buddhist community is less likely to work in the secular world. For instance, would a male servant be superior to his female employer? Would a male chauffeur be nobler than a female president? In a secular world where those who are older and wiser are respected, it would be disgraceful to ask mothers or grandmothers to kneel down and prostrate themselves to their sons or grandsons, as this would be a total violation of ethical norms. Nevertheless, in conservative monasteries, even a senior female monk, no matter how long she has been fully ordained, is supposed to prostrate herself before novice male monks.

Here we can see the ball rolling down the slope again. Not only do monastic women suffer from prejudice in spiritual communities like sanghas, but women in the secular world are also affected. I was once at a funeral where a group of people was entering the funeral hall to pay their respects collectively to the deceased. In that moment, the host of the funeral, a bhikkhu, suddenly shouted, "Men in the front, women in the back!" This abrupt instruction made a grandma who was walking in the front panic. She turned around and pushed her grandson in front of her. I witnessed that absurd circumstance and was dumbfounded. I wanted to protest but knew it would be improper to do so on such an occasion, so I gave up.

Sixth, in all kinds of religions, monks or clergy who observe celibacy tend to vilify women or create regulations that confine and belittle women. Buddhists are no better than Catholics in this regard. As a matter of fact, the majority of religious sexual scandals are committed by men. To offer a reasonable explanation, we can say that men find it harder to resist seduction than women. In the face of strong temptation, men do not surrender but fight with full strength, which makes them treat women like enemies or demons. Naturally, emotions like fear or hatred arise. When men exaggerate and distort the image of women, not only does it serve as a form of venting, but the abominable distortion of mental female images can also serve as an effective aid to meditation against (sexual) desire. This helps to strengthen their resistance to temptation. I can certainly empathize with their vulnerability, embarrassment, and pain. Nonetheless, having empathy does not necessarily mean that I support their self-justified behaviors of shaming and denigrating women. Their concepts and techniques to deal with their inner demons cannot be regarded as acts based on ultimate truth.

SINGER: I appreciate your insightful analysis on the reasons why religious institutions so often place women in an inferior position. I have not had much to contribute to this dialogue, because in regard to the position of women in Buddhism and other religious institutions, you know much more than I do. I do want to note, however, that utilitarians have long been at the forefront of the movement for equality between the sexes. In 1866 John Stuart Mill was elected to Parliament on a platform that included the radical idea of allowing women to vote. He presented a petition on that issue, which led to the first parliamentary debate on equality for women. His motion to allow women to vote was defeated, as he knew it would be, but the fact that it was supported by seventy-three members of the House of Commons was immensely encouraging for the female suffrage movement.

Mill's thinking about the position of women was greatly influenced by his long-term friend and later wife, Harriet Taylor. His pioneering essay "On the Subjection of Women" was published after her death, but he acknowledges his enormous debt to her and also the assistance of her daughter (his stepdaughter) Helen Taylor. Mill also campaigned for married women to be allowed to own property, because in his time, when a woman married, all her property lawfully became the property of her husband.

Henry Sidgwick, a later nineteenth-century English utilitarian, was a professor at Cambridge University, which back then had only male students. In 1871, together with his wife, Eleanor Sidgwick, he established a hall of residence for women so they could attend lectures at the university. Incredibly, it was not until 1948 that Cambridge allowed women to receive degrees.

You are closer to the utilitarian ethical view than the Buddhists and other religious leaders who defend the inferiority of women. I wish you success in the long struggle for complete equality between women and men—and also for those who do not identify as either sex.

CHAO-HWEI: Your acknowledgment is very meaningful and encouraging to me. It feels like utilitarianism and Buddhism share a similar perspective; both of them value the physical and mental experience of eliminating suffering and attaining happiness. No, it is certainly not enough to fight only for women's equality. In this world, there are many other gender identities, including gay, lesbian, transgender, and some nonbinary individuals who need more time and space to explore their gender identities (LGBTQIA+). I will continue to stand by them and support the movement of gender equality with the Buddhist perspective.

CHAPTER 4

Sexuality

SINGER: I noticed in one of your writings that you talk about "liberation from sex," and I thought this would be an interesting topic for us to discuss. The idea that sex is something from which we should be liberated needs, in my view, some explaining and a defense.

Before I invite you to give that explanation and defense, however, let me say something about how I regard this topic. Christianity has long had a negative view of sexuality except in relation to marriage. In the Roman Catholic tradition, sex is only permitted within a marriage and is always supposed to be open to procreation, so the use of contraception is not permitted.

When I was growing up in Australia in the 1950s and early 1960s, sex was widely seen as one of the most important moral issues. When leading conservative community figures, especially religious leaders, talked about a "decline in morals," they usually were referring to people having sex with someone to whom they were not married. It was generally considered wrong to have sex outside marriage or at least outside a close, loving relationship of the kind that was likely to lead to marriage. This caused hardship and anxiety for single people. Women suffered the most because the prevailing sexual morality was extremely sexist. Men were not blamed for having a one-night stand with a woman—this was just "sowing their wild oats"—but if a woman did it, she was thought of as a "slut," a very derogatory term that gave a woman a reputation that was widely regarded as shameful.

Attitudes toward sex began to change with the advent of the contraceptive pill in the mid-1960s. Today the prevailing ethic in the West is not opposed to people having sex with any consenting adult partner simply because they want to do it. Of course, there are exceptions among conservative Christians and some other religious groups, but for most people, sex is not seen as a big moral issue anymore.

There has been an even more dramatic change in views of same-sex relationships in recent decades. In the 1960s sodomy was illegal in many Western countries, and even when it was decriminalized, many people still thought it was "perverted." Now most people—again with the exception of religious conservatives—regard it as no different, morally, from sexual intercourse between a man and a woman, and the recent acceptance of same-sex marriage effectively puts that equality into law. I welcome these changes, because the utilitarian view is that if people enjoy having sex and freely consent to it, then there isn't anything wrong with it. That brings me to the question to which I would like you to respond: if sex is not wrong, why do people need to be liberated from it?

CHAO-HWEI: Let me see if I understand the most important question about sexual liberation. From the utilitarian perspective, it's not a bad thing if those taking part really enjoy it, because then there's nothing wrong with it. So how does this relate to your question about sexual liberation?

SINGER: It's not about sexual liberation—that would have a very different meaning—at least in English. Sexual liberation would mean liberation from sexual repression. But the expression in the English translation of your book *Buddhist Normative Ethics* is "liberation from sex." That would normally be understood to mean that you are liberated by *not* having sex or perhaps by not having the desire for sex. Liberation from sex therefore seems to be connected to celibacy. It suggests that there is something desirable about being free of sexual desires and therefore appears to resemble the traditional Christian view that we would be better off if we did not have such desires.

I am not saying that this is the standard Christian view today—many Christians take a different view. But it can be traced back to early Christian texts. Paul, for example, said that it would be better if unmarried people and widows stayed unmarried, as he did, although he added that if they cannot control themselves, they should marry, because it is "better to marry than to burn." These words were generally taken to mean that if you did not marry, you might sin by having sex outside marriage, and then you would burn in hell. More recent translations render Paul's words as "burn with passion," which gives a different connotation to the comment. (I don't know which is the more accurate version.[1])

CHAO-HWEI: This ambivalent response to sex has been around for a long time. On the one hand, sex as a concept is fatally attractive. It can be so attractive or so fascinating that a person is willing to submit to that kind of pleasure and desire; yet this is the very thing they fear the most, because this is the circumstance in which they will feel the least amount of control. This is why they will feel an ambivalent response between strongly desiring it and enjoying it and feeling deep resentment and fear. It is beyond their control.

Before contraceptive measures were available, when people had heterosexual sex, normally it would result in pregnancy, and with pregnancy came the problem of to whom the children belong—the father's side or the mother's side. Therefore, to maintain a social order, there are protocols for sex. Even if we disregard the opinions of religious groups, as a society we have to choose how to regulate to whom children belong. In general, whether it is a patriarchal or matriarchal society, to some extent there should be a way to determine who has the responsibility of raising the offspring.

The majority of societies throughout history became more patriarchal as they developed. A patriarchal society will typically decide that where the sperm comes from is the decisive factor in where the child belongs, so they need to ensure that the sperm that creates the children actually comes from the man who will fill the role of father to the children. To ensure this purity of the patriarchal lineage, women are required to remain chaste. Then the patriarchal lineage will be willing to raise the children. As a result, the tradition of establishing who the father is limits how we picture the family.

For the image of a family to remain fixed—one father with one mother, or a father with many mothers—the loyalty of women is paramount. If we consider children as property, without a doubt they belong to the father's family. Following this logic, it is obvious that when a son is born, the family can expect a daughter-in-law to bring them grandchildren. However, if a girl is born, she will become someone else's daughter-in-law. In terms of property, a daughter is less "economical," which degrades women's status.

Nevertheless, there is an alternative in human society, such as the matriarchal society of Mosou, a small ethnic group living on the border between Yunnan and Sichuan Provinces in China.

They practice "walking marriage"; the wife and husband do not live in the same household. After a woman gives birth, the father does not have to be responsible for raising their child. Instead, the woman's brothers take on the role of father in the child's life. Under this kind of social structure, a woman does not necessarily have only one sexual partner, and she may not be so concerned about who the child's father is. A woman can have many sexual partners without ethical controversy. Certainly this does not mean she *must* have multiple sexual partners, but it is possible for her. Due to such possibilities, a society like this places a lot less restriction on female chastity than patriarchal societies do.

Religions born out of patriarchal societies can hardly avoid the influence of patriarchal thinking. For example, a well-developed consciousness of gender equality in a society may be evidenced by valuing marital faithfulness for both men and women equally and reinforcing monogamy. Still, the purpose of marriage is to procreate and regulate the responsibilities and obligations for raising offspring. Generally, the offspring from a marriage belong to the man and bear his family name rather than that of the mother. In addition, while both cultural norms and religious institutions advocate faithfulness in marriage for both genders, in practice, women's fidelity is always more strictly required than men's.

SINGER: You have set out very well the problem I was talking about. Religion comes out of an earlier period, often—and certainly in the case of Christianity—a more strongly patriarchal period, as well as one without reliable contraception. Then religious doctrines from that era had the effect of petrifying morality at that pre-contraceptive stage, turning it into commandments carved in stone that are very difficult to change. An ethic that is open to reason and argument is less committed to past traditions and can change more easily when circumstances change. I know that you are very willing to interpret Buddhist traditions in a way that is in keeping with modern thinking and the problems our world faces today, so I wonder whether you are not also willing to interpret Buddhist views on sex in a way that is not subject to patriarchal influences and takes account of the availability of modern contraception?

CHAO-HWEI: First of all, there has been an emphasis on the correlation between love and sex since ancient times, which could be problematic. For most spouses, it is true that love and sex are symbiotic, but sex workers and their clients may really only have sex without love. Contraception is certainly significant since it solves the problem of whom offspring belong to and who is responsible for raising children. With this understanding, we can think about the Buddhist perspective on sex and love.

Self-love can generate a form of "attachment to self," cherishing one's own body, especially the satisfaction of physical senses. Five kinds of desire are associated with the five sense organs (eyes, ears, nose, tongue, and skin). These desires arise from self-love, which is actually instinctual. Due to self-love, a person wishes for a certain kind of state that provides sensory satisfaction. When hunger arises, one needs to eat; when thirst arises, one needs to drink. If one seeks the satisfaction of sensuous or physical needs, there will not be a moral judgment as long as the person does not hurt others. But among the five physical desires, sexual desire has been looked on more sternly since the ancient times.

It's easy to talk about how we treat our desire for food, for example, but we cannot really adopt this kind of easy attitude when we talk about sexual desire, because sex involves another person. If both people feel that having sex is just like finishing a meal, then there should be no problem. But we cannot always expect that to be the situation, even when using the example of animals. For a female cat to allow a male cat to approach is not easy.

Once there was a male cat on the college campus, and he looked so gorgeous that when a movie star saw a picture of him, she immediately liked him because of how "spiritual" he looked. She wanted her female cat to mate with that male cat, so she brought her cat to the college personally. The whole day, the other venerables at the college and I saw how the male cat tried to chase the female cat without success. Neither cat could rest properly during that whole night and the next day. We felt pity for the male and also for the female, who was trying to avoid the male and run away. In this case, we only saw the suffering of the male cat's unsatisfied desire and the female's constant need to escape from the male, but there was no sin. After two days of chasing, they both ran out of energy, and they just sat down and looked at each other in exhaustion.

If we take this example and look at human society, we will see that under normal circumstances, there is a kind of distance between people, as there was with the two cats. Unless there is a sense of security, it's not easy to diminish that sense of distance. It is a lot more complicated than just having a meal and satisfying one's own appetite. The satisfaction of human sexual desire should happen within a secure environment with the consent by both parties rather than one side ravaging the other. Even in the business relationship between a sex worker and a client, there should be this level of balance. So the Buddhist perspective on sexual desire is that it is an extension of instinctual self-love and does not necessarily involve morality.

Nevertheless, as soon as it involves the suffering of others, it is a different case.

SINGER: What you said about sexual desire manifesting self-love reminds me of a line by Woody Allen in one of his movies where he talks about masturbation and says, "Masturbation is sex with someone you love." But I mention masturbation not only to relate this joke, but because you are saying that you can't treat sexuality like a meal because you need a partner. Masturbation is one sexual act where you don't need to have a partner. Despite this, the Christian, or again more specifically the Roman Catholic, view of masturbation is negative because it says that it is a misuse of the genital organs, which are intended for the purpose of procreation. The orthodox Jewish view is the same, based on the biblical condemnation of Onan for spilling his seed on the ground.[2] So again, I wonder whether the Buddhist view shares this notion that masturbation is sinful because it's not a proper use of the body, or whether it takes a different view.

CHAO-HWEI: Buddhism is primarily concerned with liberation from suffering rather than satisfaction of desires. So as long as the pursuit of sexual satisfaction does not inflict suffering and there are safe boundaries, we do not condemn it or make a moral judgment about it. However, if one harms oneself for sexual satisfaction, it is a more complicated issue that involves personal value. Therefore, I will not dive into that discussion. We will only talk about sexual activity that involves another person. If another party is harmed physically or mentally, or the sex happens without consent, then it involves morality, even laws. Masturbation typically does not harm another person or even involve another person, so from the Buddhist perspective, there is no moral issue here. Nevertheless, masturbation is another form of satisfying self-desire. We do not judge it morally, but at the same time we are cautious because it is associated with the satisfaction of self-love; if that desire is not satisfied, then suffering will arise. Buddhism is more concerned with this consequence.

SINGER: I'm not really sure what the concern is, so if you don't mind, may I inquire further? What exactly is the consequence Buddhists are concerned about? Is it merely that you are giving in to a physical desire?

CHAO-HWEI: Buddhism is concerned about the suffering that would be caused by sexual desire; this suffering is a difficult struggle. On the one hand, if sensuous desires are not satisfied, then one will feel dissatisfied, which itself is already a form of suffering. Even once one's sensuous desires are satisfied, one very quickly turns from a feeling of happiness to one of numbness or even to a sense of loss or displeasure. The pursuit of sexual satisfaction can dull our sensory perception. Taking satisfaction in food as an example, we may enjoy the first bite of a dish but lose that pleasure by the tenth bite. As for the satisfaction of desire, initially, as long as it does not involve the suffering of others and can ease one's own suffering from desperation, there is a positive value in pursing one's desire in terms of eliminating suffering and gaining happiness. However, on a deeper level, if one's life pursuit fixates on the satisfaction of desires, it will be impossible to escape from this cycle of suffering—one's senses are first aroused and excited, then they turn numb. The result might be that we try to increase the intensity of stimulation; we bring in more of what satisfies our sensuous desires, or we change the ways we fulfill those desires.

We feel less guilty with the variety of food we choose to eat. If we try to satisfy desire by increasing the variety of tasty foods we eat, then it is possible we will start to crave foods with stronger tastes, such as saltier or spicier foods, which may result in the deterioration of our health. At least, the scope of this influence is only on the personal health level. On the other hand, when it is sexual desire we are talking about, a similar desire for variety does involve another person, and so it can raise moral issues, and guilt will sometimes be more appropriate. In Chinese we have a saying that the wife cannot be compared to the concubine, and the concubine cannot be compared to going out and having a secret sexual affair. That is because those who do this are actually trying to intensify the stimulation or are changing partners for variety.

Let's suppose that both partners in a relationship are willing to explore various forms of sexual intercourse and enjoy ways of intensifying arousal and stimulation. On the surface, it might seem that both men and women are sexually liberated, which does have some value, because this challenges the biased, moral, cultural norms, according to which women should not seek sexual pleasure. However, if we observe closely, we will discover that as couples keep indulging in increasing varieties and intensities of pleasure-seeking, they can become slaves to desire. What seems like sexual liberation is, after all, just an illusion covering the fact that people allow themselves to be dominated and bound by desire.

As a result, we see different choices in this world. Most people do not choose monastic lives, knowing they cannot rise beyond desire and sex, but they may live happy and satisfying lives in monogamous relationships. Nevertheless, some have different preferences; for example, they might prefer one-night stands or sadomasochistic experiences. In these cases, when both parties agree to and want it, we can put the moral issue aside. However, because these people are actually bound by desire, this is actually suffering for both parties. It may seem they are seeking liberation, but actually they put themselves into a deeper trap or shackle of desire and are not really "liberated." I wonder which way heterosexual men would feel more at ease. To be in control of their desire and not aroused even if women approach and flirt with them, or simply following their animal instincts and always paying attention to the opposite sex?

SINGER: Is this then a specific example of what we were talking about in more general terms this morning, when I questioned the Buddhist goal of nirvana, or release from the cycle of life, and asked if it was not one-sided to focus only on relief from suffering? If you become like the man who, as you said, is not aroused by the woman flirting with him, then you will not suffer from sexual desire anymore, but you will also lose out on the pleasure and excitement of fulfilling sexual desire. You asked me which man is more at ease, and it's true that the man who is not aroused is more at ease, but that is not the only relevant question. If the next day you were to ask which man had the more exciting evening, or which man had the most pleasure and enjoyment, then it's very likely to be the man who was aroused. At least, that would be so if the woman was attracted to him and willing to go to bed with him. So once again, the question is whether when we eliminate suffering, we are not eliminating sources of joy and happiness as well.

CHAO-HWEI: This is a very interesting question! I have a well-known Chinese anecdote to tell. In the Ming dynasty there was a very talented and accomplished scholar called Tang Bohu, who was a great artist in calligraphy and painting. One day he met a beautiful woman, Chiu-Hsiang, who was a maid serving in the household of a very prosperous government official. He was so attracted to her that he was willing to sell himself out to become a servant to that family in order to get close to the woman he admired.

When the prosperous family found out that their new servant was the accomplished scholar, they were very pleased and agreed to let the maid marry this man. This anecdote reminds us of the "happily ever after" ending for the prince and princess in folklore. But if you actually examine the biographical documentation about Tang Bohu, you will discover that before this maid there were several other women, and also after this maid there were several other women. So if we keep striving to achieve sensual pleasure, then we will be caught up in the cycle of intensifying or changing the stimulation for the sake of variety. Although one might feel that this is a happy life, if one really observes one's own body and mind, one would realize that this constant stimulation is actually a kind of suffering. The Buddha adopted two levels of teaching regarding the satisfaction of sexual desire: one is to satisfy all your desires as long as you do not harm others, and the other is the exercise of self-control, which means that you avoid becoming addicted to the need for intense stimulation or chasing after new varieties of pleasure.

To understand the Buddha's teaching on a more advanced level, it may help if I refer to a dialogue I had a few years ago with the German monk Father Anselm Grün[3] and Ms. Wu Hsin-Ru, a Christian who was our translator. I spoke to her about the idea of attaining a certain stage of meditative absorption called *prasrabhi*. She had a hard time comprehending this concept and did not know how to translate it. It is a Mahayana Buddhist term translated as "pliancy," "flexibility," or "alertness." It is defined as the ability to apply body and mind toward virtuous activity. This word simply describes a state beyond what we commonly know as happiness or excitement. It is a state of repose, refreshment, and serenity. A quality shared by all stages of meditative absorption is the letting go of desires. It happens spontaneously, rather than forcing oneself to let go while still having strong desires.

For meditators who have reached the first stage of meditative absorption, excitement is actually gross perception and makes them suffer. It's not that a person should suppress themself to the point of not having these desires and the pleasure of their satisfaction or should live a boring life. Rather, they are quite aware of the suffering inflicted by physical excitement and therefore seek more true joy in dhyana or meditation.

To sum up, sex is an animal instinct. If a sexual act does not involve hurting or harassing other beings, it has nothing to do with morality. But sexual desire falls under the big umbrella of desires. Any yearning from desire triggers suffering, which is why the Buddha's teaching focuses on alleviating and transcending suffering. The teachings guide us to the path of meditative absorption, or wisdom, as a way of letting go of desire.

SINGER: Does it follow that if you want to get to the highest stage of dhyana, that's not compatible with engaging in sexual relationships?

CHAO-HWEI: Maybe it can be put in this way: successful meditators do not necessarily feel that they have to force themselves to forgo the excitement of sensual stimulation. They do not put a moral judgment on themselves and say, "No. I have to refrain from the yearning of sensual stimulation." They just naturally stop having that yearning. Yearning triggers suffering, and they do not pursue suffering.

SINGER: I hope that if you are introducing one person in a relationship to this form of meditation, you will also introduce the other one, because otherwise it could damage the relationship. If one person in the relationship goes through these stages and ceases to have any physical desire for the other, while the other person does not go through these stages and still has them, the person who retains the physical desires will have been harmed.

CHAO-HWEI: Certainly, at the beginning, both of them will be on the same frequency. Then maybe one of them starts to transcend, and the other stays within the same sphere as they were previously. If they continue to live together, then neither of them will be happy. In this situation, if there is both sex and love between the two of them, they will really need to discuss whether they should go on and transcend the physical pleasures together and enjoy the same kind of joy. Or if the other person is against doing that, perhaps they should separate.

SINGER: Thank you for this explanation of the Buddhist perspective on "liberation from sex." As I now understand it, there is no necessary incompatibility with a utilitarian view. Everything depends on our judgment of the balance between pleasure and suffering when people are sexually active and the pleasures of a life in which desire has been transcended. If it is true that, as you said a moment ago, the pleasures of transcending desire bring in more joy than the physical pleasures, then utilitarians would also have to favor transcending desire. Utilitarians might then ask further questions about whether it would be bad if no one had sex anymore and our species died out, but that is a separate question.

I would now like to shift the focus of our discussion to a different issue, though still in the area of sex. As I mentioned earlier, in most Western countries now, couples of the same sex can legally get married. I understand that you conducted a Buddhist wedding ceremony for a lesbian couple in Taiwan, although same-sex marriage was not yet legal in Taiwan. Did you get any negative reactions here for conducting a wedding ceremony for a lesbian couple? What is the thinking of other Buddhists on this question?

CHAO-HWEI: In Buddhism, at least according to the scriptures, we cannot find passages saying that sexual relations between people of the same sex are sinful or that only heterosexual unions are acceptable. We don't really have such words. The only differentiation of moral standard we would make would be based, not on sex or gender differences, but on whether we harm others. The Buddhist view of morality is, in this respect, different from the Christian view. We do not impose the category of "sins" on sexual acts that do not harm others, so when it comes to consensual sexual relations, we do not label such acts as sinful or not.

After I officiated the wedding for the lesbian couple, I had support from some Buddhists. Although some of them said nothing publicly, they showed their support in private. But of course, we could see on the Internet that some people strongly objected to what I did. Those critical objections would not be the mainstream of Buddhist thinking, though.

I see this response as connected to the way that Buddhism sees sex, which is that it judges it more as a product of lust and desire and whether it harms others rather than whether it is between people of the opposite or the same sex. Here in Taiwan, there have been different discussions about legalizing same-sex marriage. In the whole spectrum of the gay rights movement, some people, especially from the gay and lesbian community, argue that we should strive for the legalization of same-sex marriage. Others say that to do this would be to repeat the same structure that has often caused problems for heterosexuals, and therefore they recognize nonmarital forms such as partnership. There is even a left wing thought that proposes to "eliminate the family structure and abolish marriages." All of them want different laws and regulations. Among them, draft legislation to recognize "multiple family formation" was proposed to allow for different family forms, in contrast to the traditional marriage system.

That proposed law was strongly objected to by the Christian community. As far as I know, right-wing Christian communities are against same-sex marriages, unmarried partnerships, and multiple family formations. More progressive denominations reluctantly accepted domestic partnership but objected to the other forms. Due to strong homophobia, gay and lesbian communities have temporarily tried to unite for a short-term legislative goal. Eventually, they came to an agreement to pursue the legalization of same-sex marriage. Even if individuals chose to remain unmarried, no one would be deprived of their right to marry. Taiwan became the first country in Asia to legalize same-sex marriage on May 24, 2019.

In Asia, especially in Taiwan, gay and lesbian groups stage very large parades and protests. From a broader perspective, gay rights movements are not just social movements for gay communities but also equal rights movements that include the larger LGBTQIA+ population. From the Buddhist point of view, I think we Buddhists should cultivate a more open-minded attitude for all forms of partnerships and family and accept many possibilities. However, we didn't expect that there would be such strong Christian opposition to it.

SINGER: What proportion of people in Taiwan are Christian?

CHAO-HWEI: Maybe only 5 percent. The proposed legislation was debated in 2013, and Christians claimed that passing it would destroy the family and lead people to abandon marriage. They believe it would challenge the fundamental value of home life and lead to the disintegration of family values. Nevertheless, they deliberately confused people and tried to make them believe that the gay community dismisses their closely held values and would like to eliminate the family structure and abandon marriage, ignoring the fact that there are gay people who value family and would like to honor its value through the same right of marriage. Some Christians organized the Family Guardian Coalition and defined *home* as a union shared only by a man and a woman, which clearly excludes same-sex couples' right to have their own families.

SINGER: This is exactly the same argument that has been used in other countries, and all the evidence suggests the opposite— namely that marriage provides more security for same-sex couples and that children brought up by same-sex couples are just as likely to be well-adjusted, happy children as children brought up by heterosexual couples.

CHAO-HWEI: More than twenty thousand participants joined the parade in 2013. The masses in this parade bore three conflicting agendas: the legalization of same-sex marriage, the system of unmarried partnership, and the multiple family formation initiative. Although they each held their own ideals, they decided to unite against the anti-gay camp and focus on advocating for the legalization of same-sex marriage. The Christians, allied with other opponents, staged an opposing parade. They were aware that they could not persuade Taiwanese people by using the Bible, so they invited representatives from other religions in Taiwan, claiming that *all* the religions in Taiwan were against the proposed legislation. But everyone knows that the main objection came from the Christian community. They managed to mobilize about sixty thousand people and avoided claiming that they were Christians. Some political representatives became worried about losing votes, so they were able to pause the progress on the proposed bill. If it were not for our president, who intended to legalize same-sex marriage and had the judicial review to break through this siege, the law would not have passed. Political representatives were too scared to lose votes from religious groups.

SINGER: The last question that I have in this area of sexism and gender discrimination is related to the recent controversy in many countries regarding recognition of people who do not wish to identify with the gender they were assigned at birth. I expect, from your answers to previous questions, that the Buddhist view is that if this does not harm anybody, then there will be no moral objection to people identifying as a gender that is not the sex they were assigned at birth. Is that right?

CHAO-HWEI: That's right, but there is more to be said. Several of the Buddha's disciples were able to transform their gender, from male to female and from female to male! Nowadays those who make this transition have help from medical technology, but apparently that was not needed in the Buddha's time. It seemed like a natural transgender process. This is recorded in the Vinaya Buddhist scriptures.

Based on what I have read in the scriptures, the Buddha did not discriminate against these individuals. He only made some regulations: if one chose to transform from male into female, then one should join the female monastic community and vice versa, though they did not need to go through the orientation ceremonies again. He did not consider being transgender as immoral or incorrect. Something that would be a cause for moral concern would be fetishism or pedophilia. These people deserve more compassion because they have no control over their desires, which leads to harm to children and others.

SINGER: Yes, I understand that. First, it's very interesting that being transgender is already there in Buddhist scriptures; I did not know that. Second, regarding the comment you made about technology, many of the people who are transgender are not actually having surgery or hormones but rather are identifying with a different sex. Trans women may dress as women, take female names, and ask you to refer to them as "she" even if they were assigned male gender at birth. Some may take hormones and perhaps eventually choose surgery, and some may do neither. Whether they want to change their physiology or their anatomy is separate from their personal identification.

CHAO-HWEI: The legal controversy here would be whether they want to go through some official recognition of their change of gender, because in Taiwan our identification cards contain a space to indicate whether you are male or female. So would transgender people go so far as to ask for their gender to be legally changed on their documentation?

SINGER: Yes, they do want to be legally recognized as the gender they identify with. Another possibility, which the Australian government has now adopted, is to have a third category of "indeterminate." This category has been used by people who are born with elements of both male and female, but it also gives everyone another option. It means that if a person arrives at a country's immigration control dressed as a woman but otherwise with male physical characteristics, their passport does not have to say that they are male or female but can say "indeterminate." That could prevent problems that might otherwise occur when the person tries to pass through immigration control.

CHAPTER 5

Embryo Research and Abortion

SINGER: Chao-Hwei, I would now like to raise a different and perhaps more contentious topic, so we can explore some of the differences, as well as the similarities, in our ethical views. In your excellent book *Buddhist Normative Ethics*, you discuss the killing of embryos in order to obtain stem cells for medical research. You say that life begins when the sperm and the egg fuse, when the sperm fertilizes the egg. As you know, Christians often take the key question to be "When does a human life begin?" They think that if a human life begins at conception, then it follows that destroying an embryo, or having an abortion, is taking an innocent human life, and they assume that it must be wrong to take an innocent human life.

I cannot agree with this Christian viewpoint, because in my view the crucial ethical question is not "Is the embryo a living human being?" but "Is the embryo the kind of being that it is always, or almost always, wrong to kill?" I do not think it is wrong to end the life of a being that has never, ever been conscious, or had the capacity to enjoy its life, or had any desires about its future. In your book you say that although the embryo does not have the capacity to feel pain or pleasure, as its sensory organs have not fully developed, this does not mean that using such embryos is not killing them. On this specific point—are we killing these embryos when we use them in research?—I agree with you. To destroy an embryo in order to obtain stem cells *is* killing a living organism. But the question I want to focus on is whether there is anything wrong with this particular act of killing. Here perhaps we disagree, because you continue by saying that Buddhists who uphold the practice of no killing cannot agree with the killing of embryos.

I would like to better understand this Buddhist practice of no killing. Plants are alive, but we do kill plants, both the plants we eat and the weeds we must destroy to allow the ones we eat to grow. If it is not wrong for us to kill plants, then the fact that we are killing a living thing cannot settle the question of whether our act is wrong. The embryo, at this early stage of its development when it might be killed to obtain stem cells, is just as incapable of feeling pain as the lettuce we were eating at lunch. If killing embryos is not different from cutting a lettuce to eat it, then is killing an embryo really something we should be objecting to?

CHAO-HWEI: We can start to answer the question by examining the cutting of lettuce. If a person develops a heightened awareness for their surroundings, they will become more aware of thriving life. The Buddha wanted monastics to neither destroy seeds that could grow into plants nor cut thriving plants, and they could not throw waste on the grass. However, the Buddha could not ban them from eating vegetables. We need always to keep in mind whether a precept is practicable; otherwise, the precepts will only cause unnecessary trouble.

In ancient India, monastics largely lived on what people put in their begging bowls, so they did not have to cut the vegetables or plants for themselves. Nevertheless, when Buddhism spread to China, the culture was unfavorable to begging and did not draw a distinction between ordinary beggars and the monastic practice of walking from place to place with a begging bowl. They challenged the ethics of the monastics because they were not involved in any labor, asking, "Why don't you cut the vegetables yourselves? Why should other people serve you?" This leads back to the previous emphasis—are precepts practical? Eventually, this criticism led the monastics in China to grow and cook their own food, which means that, as much as we want to protect plants, it would be impossible to sustain our lives without using them.

An important distinction, though, is that we *can* survive without eating animals. That is why I am opposed to the argument "Since you already eat vegetables, and it is a kind of killing, you should not stop me from killing animals." It is impossible to refrain 100 percent from cutting or killing vegetables, but this is not a reason to support killing animals or embryos. If we look at embryos like plants and believe we can cut them up or kill them because they do not feel pain, then can we also kill anesthetized babies or adults because they, too, do not feel pain? The answer is obviously no. The point is, just because a student cannot achieve 100 percent perfection, this does not mean they should just submit a blank paper. The student could always do their best, instead of making an all-or-nothing choice between an A+ or a fail. In the same vein, life is more than a game that offers merely two choices: A+ or fail. Just because we cannot avoid regret from harming and consuming vegetables does not mean we can extend this harm to the killing of embryos and other animals. We cannot treat this issue with an all-or-nothing mindset.

SINGER: I totally agree with you about this argument that because we must eat plants that were alive but have been killed for us, we might as well eat animals too. It's a bad argument.

CHAO-HWEI: We need to clarify this and not just compare and contrast killing an embryo to cutting lettuce. All moral principles should be rooted in practicality. People may have a clearer awareness of what they are doing when they are cutting lettuce than they have when they are killing an embryo because it takes some kind of scientific knowledge or technological equipment to understand the condition of an embryo. So people's awareness and feelings for the embryo will be less than they have for living things of which they have direct experience, like lettuce.

Most people do not have feelings for embryos. That makes dissecting embryos an even more complex ethical issue to discuss than killing animals. It's a discussion that will only be conducted among elite medical and biological scientists and scholars in ethics. With the help of equipment that enables us to observe the strong survival instinct of embryos, empathy is possible. This equipment can also help the general public better understand embryos and expand the scope of their experiences. If people claim that they cannot feel the pain of chickens being bred and slaughtered, then we can show them a video of factory farming and of chickens having their throats cut, and they'll become aware of how chickens suffer. Likewise, we can do the same for embryos with the help of technology. Where does the difficulty lie? It turns out that current scientific evidence is not favorable to proving or justifying the protection of embryos. Scientists claim that an embryo within fourteen days of conception is not yet capable of feeling pain. That is obviously not favorable evidence for protecting embryos or preventing them from being killed.

On this issue, Buddhist sayings are similar to those of modern science. You can find it recorded in Buddhist texts that we think that for the first fourteen days after conception, when the embryo is being formed, it has not developed the capacity to feel pain yet. From the day of conception until day 226—before a baby is born (less than nine months)—the Buddhist scripture calculates 7 days as one unit and divides the 266 days into thirty-eight stages of 7 days. For the first 7 days, the embryo consists of drops of fluid and is described as *kalala* in Sanskrit. For the second 7 days, it is called *arbuda* and has become a gelatinous ball—an embryo not yet capable of feeling pain. Over the course of the third set of 7 days, it is shaped like a lump of soft flesh and is called *pesi*. According to this description, even 21 days after conception, an embryo still lacks the function of neurotransmission; thus, it certainly cannot feel pain when it is less than 14 days old.[1]

SINGER: May I interrupt here? I presume you are referring to a very old sutra here, and it seems extraordinary that ancient writers could have had such a broadly correct understanding of the development of the early embryo. How did they know anything about the formation of the early embryo inside a woman's body? Were postmortem examinations performed on women who died early in pregnancy?

CHAO-HWEI: That's an interesting question, and your interruption is very welcome. The sutra is indeed very ancient. It was translated into Chinese in the eighth century C.E., but it is an assembly of different texts that were written in different periods over some centuries before that.

How then did the ancients know anything about the early development of the fetus inside a woman's body? The answer is that those who achieve meditative stillness and insight will also develop the power to gain a clear vision, not only of their own bodies but also those of others. Therefore, they would not need to obtain this knowledge by means of postmortem examinations performed on women.

Now, to return to the ethical question we were discussing. From the Buddhist perspective, how do we prove that the value of an embryo of at least fourteen days will be equal to the value of a formed baby with a head and limbs or a baby that is already born? From either a Buddhist perspective or a scientific perspective, whether we are discussing an embryo, a fetus, or a baby, there are indeed differences that take place during the process of development. As a result, it is understandable that people's moral responses or feelings are different if we are talking about the removal of an embryo, the abortion of a formed fetus, or the killing of a baby. If we base our principles of not killing solely on whether the embryo can feel pain, then to say we ought not to kill the early embryo would be problematic.

There is, however, another angle that is worth our attention, especially when you look at it from the Buddhist perspective for ethical judgment. If we argue that we may destroy the embryo because it does not feel pain, that would lead to the following conclusion: as long as animals do not feel pain, we can do whatever we want with them, including killing them. This would also apply to patients who are in a coma. If a patient does not feel pain, can we just kill them? We are trying to promote animal welfare and protection and will not accept a conclusion like this. Some Christians claim that embryos have a kind of moral status, which means that only God can decide if they live or die. From this view, humans should not deny embryos the right to life. Since Buddhism does not have a belief that supports creationism as Christianity does, it is hard to support an argument against the usage of embryos with this kind of theological approach. However, we still try to encourage scientists to find a better way of obtaining stem cells to cure diseases. By that, of course, I mean a way of obtaining stem cells that does not involve killing embryos for our use. Scientists should seriously consider other alternatives.

Meanwhile, we want to acknowledge that even though early embryos do not feel pain, they nevertheless have a strong instinct for survival. The survival instinct within the embryo will cause it to keep developing until it takes shape and becomes a full-grown baby within the womb. We should therefore ask: do we really need to use embryos to the same extent that we need to eat vegetables in order to survive? If we did, we would have common ground for both using embryos and eating vegetables. There is, however, no comparison between our need to use embryos and our need to eat vegetables.

If we do not insist on the need to find alternatives to the use of embryos, and we accept the argument that because embryos cannot feel pain, they may be killed, then the same argument could support the use of animals in experiments. Scientists will claim that they will reduce the pain that the animals experience—or even that the animals will not feel pain at all. Then they will say they are justified in doing whatever they wish with anesthetized animals who will not suffer. Or some may argue that we can kill someone as long as we make sure they don't feel pain.

SINGER: Thank you for this explanation of your views. The debate about embryo experimentation in the United States is very much based on the idea that it's a *human* life, and human lives have a special moral status or an inviolable right to life. You and I are in agreement that whether killing is wrong should not depend on whether it's a human life that is at stake. So what does it depend on? One plausible answer is that it depends on whether a being is capable of feeling pain or, conversely, of enjoying its life.

You brought up two examples of beings whom you think it would be wrong to kill, namely animals and patients in a coma. To address the question of animals first, we agree that they can suffer and that if you perform experiments that cause them to suffer, then their suffering is something bad (although as we agreed at the outset of our discussion, that does not necessarily mean it is wrong to cause it, for the good consequences of doing it may, in particular circumstances, outweigh the bad). But what about experiments on animals that do not cause them to suffer in any way? Let's suppose that in order to advance our understanding of some treatment of a disease, animals are bred and reared in conditions that meet all their needs, both physical and psychological. Assume that the animals are enjoying their lives. After a few months, however, the day comes when they are ready for the experiment. They are anesthetized, and while they are under anesthetic, an experiment is performed on them. Then they are killed while still under the anesthetic, so they feel nothing more. Is that wrong? This example isolates the question of killing from the question of suffering. Remember, too, that these animals were bred specifically to be experimented on; otherwise, they would not have existed at all. Is a pleasant life and then a painless, though premature, death worse than not living at all? I find it difficult to say that it is.

Now let us consider human patients in a coma and assume that we are talking about patients who will never recover consciousness. In these circumstances, the main reason for keeping such patients alive would seem to be respect for who they were before they ceased to be conscious and respect for what they wanted—or would have wanted—to be done if they were ever to lose consciousness irreversibly. If they would have wanted to be kept alive, that is a reason for keeping them alive, but if they would have preferred not to be kept alive in that situation, that is a reason for ending their lives. Speaking personally, I would not want to be kept alive if it were clear that I would never recover consciousness, so obviously we are not justified in assuming that everyone in that state would want to continue to live. Embryos, however, have no "before"; that is, they have no past in which they were conscious and could form a preference about what they would want to happen to them. So the reason I just mentioned for keeping a patient alive, despite an irreversible loss of consciousness, cannot apply to embryos. That's why I do not see anything objectionable about the killing of an embryo at an early stage at which it clearly is not capable of feeling any pain or having any desires about its future.

If this all sounds rather complicated, the central point I am trying to make is that I regard whether a being can feel pain and suffer, or can feel pleasure and enjoy life, as crucial for whether the being has the kind of moral status that makes it morally significant. When I say that a being is morally significant, that means there are things you might do to that being that are wrong because it is worse *for that being* than something else you might do. Any being capable of feeling pain is morally significant because by causing them to suffer pain, you make things worse for them. Such a being is a subject of experiences, and therefore we can say that things go well or badly from its subjective point of view. If, on the other hand, a being cannot feel pain and is not a subject of experiences, I don't see it as having a moral status that makes it wrong to end its life. Therefore, I don't think it is wrong to kill an embryo, even if the killing is not essential for our survival.

I accept that there may be some alternative methods by which we can obtain stem cells without killing embryos. Scientists can decide whether those alternative methods will produce results that are as good as those we can get by taking stem cells from embryos. But if for some reason these alternative methods are less likely to achieve useful results than using stem cells obtained by killing embryos, I do not object to the scientists killing the embryos.

CHAO-HWEI: From all of this insightful disquisition, you have brought out various issues.

First of all, those experiments that would not subject animals to any pain seem theoretically impeccable. However, if we could equally apply ethical empathy to animals, have they *consented to* our doing these experiments on them? At present, in the field of science and ethics, researchers have unanimously agreed that experiments on humans should respect the principle of fully informing those being experimented on and having their consent. Therefore, while animals are not aware of, nor have really agreed to, these experiments, and even though they do not feel pain during the process of death because of anesthesia, aren't we guilty of ethical negligence in stealing their lives away? Doesn't it make us fall into the mentality of human chauvinism?

Returning to the issue of embryos, you say that they have no past in which they were conscious and could form a preference about what they would want to happen to them, but according to Buddhism, embryos do have a series of deaths and rebirths in the past. The general public, however, does not have the insight of knowing about these "past lives" and "future lives" and is unable to verify whether these ideas are true or false. To me, the lack of consciousness of previous lives does not fully justify the killing of embryos.

So do you think that during the first fourteen days after the embryo is formed, it is not able to feel pain and therefore it is okay to kill the embryo and use it?

SINGER: That's correct. In fact, I think it takes much more than fourteen days for the embryo or fetus to become capable of conscious experiences. Whatever we conclude about that, however, my view is that, provided one has the consent of the man and woman from whose sperm and egg the embryo was created, it is permissible to kill the embryo and use it during the period before it becomes conscious.

CHAO-HWEI: And what about the patients in severe comas or persistent vegetative states (PVS)? You seem to be distinguishing these cases because before these patients fell into a coma or PVS, they were capable of experiencing pain. Does that mean you feel it's not right to kill those people even if they do not feel pain?

SINGER: That depends on what the people themselves would have wanted. If I say, "If I am ever in a state where I have irreversibly lost consciousness, I do not want to go on living," then I think it is okay to kill me if I am later in that situation.

CHAO-HWEI: So it depends on the prior will of the patient and not merely on the fact that the patient was once conscious?

SINGER: That's right. We should honor the past will of the person if we can. If doing so requires scarce resources that could be better used to save the lives of people who can make a full recovery, however, then that would outweigh the importance of honoring the past desires of someone who cannot recover.

CHAO-HWEI: If we base our ethical judgment on the will of the patient before the patient falls into a severe coma or PVS, then we will have to deal with another related problem: what if the person really has a strong will to die? Then there will be a conflict between the will that appears on the surface and the potential survival instinct. Which one should we regard as decisive?

SINGER: If the patient was able to make a rational decision and expressed a wish to die if there were to be an irreversible loss of consciousness, I would act in accordance with the rational will, not with the biologically driven survival instinct.

CHAO-HWEI: There is a fundamental difference in our views here—you are not against killing embryos in order to use them; however, I feel otherwise.

As I understand the position you advocate in your book *Animal Liberation*, it is based on the capacity of animals to feel pain—animals can suffer, so ethically we should take into account their suffering and their happiness. Instead of ignoring the needs of animals, we have to consider the benefits for both humans and animals. In the case of a patient who has irreversibly lost consciousness, however, you hold that, in spite of the fact that they no longer feel pain, it would not be right to take the life of that patient if they previously expressed the will to continue living in that state. Newborn babies, on the other hand, are not aware of their existence and so cannot wish to continue to live, but they are capable of feeling pain. Embryos are capable of neither feeling pain nor of wishing to continue to live. You think that this makes it acceptable to use them in research.

SINGER: That is correct. In fact, I would be prepared to end the life of an embryo a lot older than fourteen days, because I would not consider that it is capable of feeling pain until there is a developed brain.

CHAO-HWEI: Then we do have different views about embryos that haven't really developed a nervous system or a brain. Scientists take for granted that they are morally justified in using embryos that haven't really developed the organs required for sentience. However, people have more ethical concerns when it is related to babies with perceptions. Let us observe the development of embryos. We can see the cells keep splitting and multiplying. This is a sort of survival instinct of embryos as "beings," even though they have not developed awareness or perception of pain at this stage. The embryo nevertheless has instincts to develop, thrive, and obtain nourishment from the mother's womb in order to continue its existence. It's just like a tiny sprout that's trying to grow into a tree with its full potential. At the experiential level, with the help of scientific equipment we can certainly see the process of an embryo striving to grow into a fetus and, eventually, a baby.

In addition, as we have already agreed, cutting and eating lettuce is necessary for our survival. Nonetheless, is there any similarly necessary reason for us to prove that we have to kill embryos? Do we have as strong a justification for killing the embryo as we have for killing the lettuce?

SINGER: Well, scientists argue that the stem cells you can get from embryos are different from the stem cells you can get from adults and that the ones you get from embryos are more likely to be useful to treat certain diseases and save lives. If they're right, then that's a very important thing to do. In a way, it's even more important than eating lettuce, because eating lettuce will only keep one person alive for a short time, whereas killing an embryo to obtain stem cells may lead to many people being saved from a disease that would otherwise kill them.

CHAO-HWEI: If we allow such logic to work here, justifying the use of embryos because of the possible benefits to many people, then scientists can also use similar arguments to defend their use of animals in experiments. From the Buddhist perspective, you can easily reach an answer by asking, "Would you like to be the embryo that is used for such experiments?"

SINGER: Well, if I were asked if I would like to be the embryo, I would have to say, "I don't mind." Because if I were the embryo, I would know nothing about it.

CHAO-HWEI: Your response illustrates the need to deepen and widen our experiences to the extent that we will be sensitive enough to observe that embryos have an instinct to survive, to grow, and to thrive. If we cultivate our experience and consciousness deeply enough, we will be able to observe that although embryos have no sentience, they strive to survive.

SINGER: We have reached an interesting point of disagreement here. If an embryo is not conscious, then I don't place any moral weight on what you are calling a survival instinct. It's true, of course, that the embryo's cells divide, and various other things happen that make it possible for the embryo to survive and develop. This is a natural process, but I don't think of it as "striving," because that term suggests a goal that is aimed at. An athlete can strive to win a race, but I don't believe that mold strives to grow on rotten fruit, nor that an embryo strives to develop into a child.

I can see that there is a sense in which we can harm a plant by cutting it down or by neglecting to water it, as a result of which it dies, and in that sense, we can harm an embryo too. But that's a very different sense from the one in which we could harm a cat by not feeding the cat and letting them die. We are causing the cat to suffer, but we do not cause the plant or the embryo to suffer. The embryo and the plant do not have states of consciousness that are worse than the states of consciousness they would have had if we had treated them differently. As I said earlier, the sense of harm to which we should give moral weight is the sense in which we cause a being to have worse states of consciousness than it would otherwise have had. This does not include thwarting what you refer to as the survival instinct of a being that has never been conscious and, if killed, never will be.

CHAO-HWEI: From the Buddhist perspective, when we give equal consideration to all sentient beings with signs of life, we especially value two instincts of life. The first is to pursue happiness and to avoid pain and suffering, and the second is to survive and avoid death. This second one is also an instinct that we should respect. In our discussion just now, I agree with what you say about the first kind of instinct, and your argument is flawless. You take the first instinct of sentient beings, which is to avoid pain and suffering and to pursue happiness, into consideration when addressing the moral weight we should give them and how we should act toward them. But when it comes to the second instinct, the survival instinct, I think your logic is flawed.

SINGER: I hope what I am about to say will not seem offensive or trivialize our discussion in any way, but among the many excellent vegan dishes that we and the other female monastics and guests had for dinner tonight was a bowl of fresh green sprouts. I ate some, and I believe that you took some too. Did you feel any kind of regret at eating perhaps fifty or one hundred sprouts? We could, after all, have nourished ourselves just as well by replacing the many sprouts with a single cabbage or, better yet, with a single squash, which we could pick and still leave the squash plant to continue to grow. Yet I did not feel that I was doing something wrong—not even a little bit wrong—in eating those sprouts. Is this a fault in me, perhaps showing my lack of sensitivity to the survival instinct of those sprouts?

CHAO-HWEI: I don't think this is offensive. Even though we agree that eating sprouts takes away their potential to grow, sprouts are different from embryos, which will later develop the capacity for feeling pain and pleasure.

After all, human life has to be sustained by food. If neither of us can bear animals' suffering when they are being raised and killed to be our food, then you and I should agree that, above all, we have to survive by eating plants. The Buddha cherished thriving lives of both animals and plants. However, the former are capable of feeling pain, while the latter are not. Therefore, though he strictly demanded that both monastic and lay disciples not kill animals, only monastics are urged to refrain from cutting grasses, woods, or seeds.

Thus, although both sprouts and embryos have the potential to survive, grow, and develop, the Buddha did not give equal moral status to embryos and vegetables.

SINGER: With the greatest respect, I do not think you have addressed the point of my example of the sprouts. Probably that is because I did not make it clearly. I referred to the sprouts, not to suggest that embryos are the same as sprouts, but to try to suggest that even you, and the others who joined in the dinner, cannot really believe that every living thing has an instinct to live and thrive, and therefore it is wrong to kill such living things for quite trivial reasons. For if you believed this, surely you would not eat—and thereby kill—one hundred living things just because you enjoy their taste or texture, when you could nourish yourself equally well with a squash that does not require you to take the life of the squash plant. To me, the simplest explanation of your willingness to eat sprouts is that you scarcely give any weight to the kind of survival instinct that is common to all living things. Your rejection of killing embryos for scientific purposes must be based on something else.

CHAO-HWEI: This is a very intriguing topic, and your doubt makes sense! Had you not brought up such a subtle question, I would have never thought of this. According to Buddhism, since we respect the survival instinct of living beings and eat vegetables to keep us alive, this no longer involves the critical issue of survival instincts of human beings. Why do Buddhist vegetarians eat bean sprouts without giving it a second thought? I am full of gratitude for your inspiration for me to think of this with more depth, and here I am trying to respond to your doubt.

Both strong sensations of pain and strong survival instincts were reasons for the Buddha to take care of animals. Then, because plants have strong survival instincts and seeds of plants have a great potential to grow, the Buddha required monastics to refrain from cutting plants as well as destroying seeds. Nevertheless, the moral status of plants is, after all, less than that of animals, because to our naked eyes plants don't suffer from strong sensations of pain. Because of this, there does not seem to be much difference between an embryo and a bean sprout.

An embryo, though, has a potential to grow into a future buddha or to grow into a person like Peter Singer who possesses logical thinking and a thoughtful mind and dedicates himself to demolishing human chauvinism and advocating for animal liberation. A bean sprout, however hard it grows, merely becomes more bean sprouts. We can seem to sense that in human minds, even though embryos are fragile and show weak signs of life, there is a more or less unsettling feeling about intentionally destroying embryos.

Buddhism talks about all lives being equal—one justification for treating sentient beings as equal is that they are capable of feeling pain and another is that they are conscious. As long as we provide them with enough education for spiritual growth, their awareness can be fully expanded, which means there is a chance for them to become a buddha or an arhat. For a bean sprout, however, there is a fundamental limit—it does not have a mind, so no matter how much it thrives, it can never become an arhat.

In the context of this chapter, I will add that when the human embryo or fetus is destroyed, they are deprived of the chance of education for spiritual growth. This is why I advocate protecting them even when they are not capable of suffering or happiness. Although the spiritual growth of normal people cannot be compared with that of enlightened ones, every ordinary person has the potential to become enlightened. Therefore the equality I refer to here does not refer to equality of status but to the potential to develop their awareness.

Most humans have a higher capacity for rationality, morality, and the exercise of their will than other animals—although there are exceptions. Nevertheless, this does not mean that animals entirely lack the potential to develop their awareness. They, like human beings, have a mind and are able to interact with others and to cultivate good qualities such as compassion and altruism. They have even been known to sacrifice themselves to help others. Plants such as bean sprouts, on the other hand, do not have a mind and therefore have no potential to develop awareness or other noble qualities.

SINGER: I agree with what you say about the differing potentials of most humans, with some exceptions, and other animals, and the lack of such a potential in plants. Nevertheless, while I agree that the embryo has the potential to develop awareness, I don't agree that this potential gives us a reason to ensure that the embryo does reach its potential. I don't see anything wrong with interrupting that potential.

CHAO-HWEI: You do not think there is a difference between sprouts and embryos?

SINGER: There are differences, and one of those differences is that the sprout has the potential to become a mature plant, and the embryo has the potential to become a mature human being. To say that we should not kill the embryo because of its potential is different from saying that we should not kill the embryo because it has an instinct to survive or is striving to develop. Nevertheless, I don't think that the argument for the potential of the embryo provides a sound reason for not killing an embryo either—at least, not in the present state of the world. If you have fertile hen eggs, and you want to have more chickens, then you will value the potential of the eggs to produce chickens more than you value the contribution the eggs might make to your breakfast. But if you don't want more chickens, you may value the eggs more when you make them into an omelet than when you allow the hen to sit on them and hatch them. Similarly, if we think it is good for the world to have as many people as possible, then it would make sense to wish that every embryo could realize its potential, but then we would also be encouraging couples to have as many children as possible. We don't do this, so I don't see why we should think it is a good thing for every embryo to develop into a mature human being.

CHAO-HWEI: Your question not only makes sense but is also powerful. It is true that the earth has limited space and resources. Not only do cats and dogs need to be neutered or spayed, but human beings also have to use birth control to prevent overpopulation. Once our population outgrows the ability of our planet to sustain us, there will be huge crises the world has to deal with, such as famine. Wars on a large scale might happen because people will fight for resources. Then we will be confronted with painful deaths of human beings rather than painless deaths of embryos. Taking bean sprouts as an example, if they grow without limitation, they might cause a big disaster for ecology. Therefore, to choose the lesser of two evils, and according to the Buddhist point of view, I am not against family planning.

We need to deepen our awareness of suffering and harm. If we go against the instinct for survival—not only the instinct for the survival of embryos but of any living beings, including animals—and even deprive them of such development, then animals will experience a strong sense of suffering, *dukkha*, for the longing to live is not satisfied or is being repressed. *Dukkha* in Buddhism refers to both suffering and harm. It turns out that suffering comes not only from awareness and resistance to pain but also from fear and desperation in the face of destruction or death. Apart from enlightened beings such as the Buddha or arhats, who have reached the level beyond self, any animal will suffer when confronted with death or destruction. Both the suffering and their resistance will remain strong, even if their nervous systems are interrupted and no longer connect to their brains and the suffering is guaranteed painless.

SINGER: Do you think that we can ascribe fear to a being without consciousness?

CHAO-HWEI: You may think that an embryo cannot feel fear. When we expand and deepen our awareness to our own mental and physical states or those of others, however, we develop keener observation. We see that when survival instincts are violated forcefully, a living organism will collapse and die with intense fear, terror, and struggle. Although an embryo is currently a living being without consciousness or the capacity to feel pain, it experiences the same level of intensity.

SINGER: I accept that if you do something to a cell, it may react in a way that can be described as defending itself from attack or trying to survive. You can see that on the biological level, but maybe we are just talking about something that is ultimately a set of complex physical and chemical reactions, without involving any intentional acts. If so, you shouldn't use the word *fear*. Fear is a mental state. If an organism is not conscious, it cannot feel fear.

CHAO-HWEI: I apologize; perhaps we need to find a better word. I was trying to say that we should give equal respect to the instinct for survival. For example, when an earthquake starts, or when everything around us is shaking, we are not hurt yet but already feel a threat of death, therefore we instinctively tremble. From microscopic observation of embryos, we realize that they are equally shaken when being killed. I think we should give equal respect to the survival instinct as much as we can, whether it happens at the level of ourselves when we are shaken by an earthquake or at the level of the cells that are shaken by a threat to their survival.

SINGER: If it's only instinct without consciousness, I don't think it is right to give it equal consideration.

CHAO-HWEI: The threat of death has an impact that is equally strong for tiny lives. There is a danger that if we cannot articulate or discuss in the public domain the reasons why embryos should be protected, then our society will accept ceaseless experiments scientists conduct with embryos and their tactful justifications. At the same time, we need to be humble and continuously deepen and expand our awareness in order to observe the potential manifestation of the embryo when it faces the threat to its survival.

SINGER: I agree that it is always good to attain more knowledge, and I certainly would encourage people to try to explore whether an embryo can, in some sense, perceive a threat and respond to it. My reading of the literature thus far is that there is no good evidence to suggest that this is the case, but I'm entirely open to doing more research on that.

In the absence of any evidence at this stage, however, what should be done? You said that the scientists will justify going ahead with research on embryos. Yes, they will, but I'm not troubled by that. It is possible that in the future we will discover evidence that shows that that was a mistake, because embryos can perceive a threat, but it is more likely, in my view, that in the future we will not find any such evidence.

CHAO-HWEI: At this stage we do not have all the evidence we need to reach that conclusion. Maybe in the future we will make new discoveries. What about between now and the future? Is it so necessary that we have to conduct such research and ignore the fundamental respect for life? Because I am concerned about the karma, or the consequences, that will be generated by the process of research using embryos before we have further discoveries. Can we reverse the thinking and ponder whether it is really necessary to use embryos to conduct stem cell research now, before there is any evidence showing that using embryos does not involve killing a living being with an instinctive desire to survive? Why don't we wait until we have more understanding and sufficient knowledge about the life signs of embryos? Or can we slow down now and show more respect for the instinctive desire for life, even if at this stage we cannot prove it scientifically?

SINGER: Yes, we could slow down, or perhaps stop altogether, research using embryos until we know more about them, but we might then be stopping research that would have saved many lives. So there is a possible cost to doing the research and a possible cost to *not* doing the research. For that reason, I would not favor the view that it would be wrong to go ahead with the research unless we are 100 percent certain that embryos cannot anticipate threats. It is extremely difficult to get 100 percent certainty, and if we make the standard for justifying research so high, we risk losing some important benefits.

I should add, though, that it may not be as essential to obtain stem cells from embryos as we once thought it was. At the time when the debate about using human embryonic stem cells was at its height in the United States in 2001, during the presidency of George W. Bush, it seemed that we could make progress only with human embryonic stem cells. Those who were opposed to using human embryos suggested that we could get stem cells from adults, but stem cells from adults have particular specialized functions, which makes them less useful than stem cells from embryos. More recently, however, it has become possible to alter adult stem cells so they become less specialized and more like the embryonic ones. My understanding is that at present we may still need some embryonic stem cells, but I would leave that question to those who are more familiar with the current state of the science than I am.[2]

CHAO-HWEI: In 2001, during the Bush government, you thought it was the right decision to develop that research?

SINGER: Yes, I think it was a reasonable decision to make at that time.

CHAO-HWEI: We need to put pressure on government so it will look for other alternatives; otherwise, it will think there are no ethical problems with taking stem cells from embryos and will just go on with these experiments without any consideration.

SINGER: Perhaps, but the importance of placing that pressure on the government depends on how much you think is on the other side of this; that is, how bad it is to destroy embryos that are not conscious to obtain stem cells. We disagree about how bad that is. I don't think there's much wrong with that, because I think it is very unlikely that these early embryos are capable of perceiving threats, and it seems reasonable to me to decide that the medical benefits outweigh the small possibility that the embryo needs to be respected.

CHAO-HWEI: But do you still think that, now that there are really alternatives to taking stem cells from embryos, as you have described? Why don't you think that we should continue pressing scientists and the government to look for other alternatives?

SINGER: Some scientists are already claiming that we've found other alternatives, and if that's correct, then we don't need to use embryos anymore. But other scientists disagree.

CHAO-HWEI: The driving force behind the search for alternatives has been ethical objections to the destruction of embryos and the pressure that this society has put on scientists and government to avoid using them. If there were enough pressure, they would then seriously consider searching for and working on alternatives for embryos.

SINGER: I cannot say what the driving force has been in Taiwan, but in the United States, the driving force behind the search for alternatives was the misguided views of Christians who believe that the embryo has a right to life because it's a human being. These Christians have no objections to taking stem cells from the embryos of nonhuman animals nor to harming conscious adult animals to obtain the embryos.

CHAO-HWEI: The Buddhist perspective values the common will of all kinds of lives—to pursue happiness and to avoid pain; to avoid death and to stay alive. Following this perspective, the moral status of embryos is justified by this common will rather than the binary division of human and nonhuman. For different reasons, both Christians and Buddhists call for scientists to find alternatives for embryos, which is good. If we have more discourse from various perspectives and more groups that are against using embryos for experiments, it might exert pressure on scientists to put more effort into finding alternatives for embryos. Otherwise, rather than finding alternatives and improving the current situation, they will just take the use of embryos for granted.

SINGER: It's getting late. We should probably take a break and get some sleep.

———

SINGER: In thinking about our discussion last night, I feel I should emphasize that although we ended on a disagreement, there is also an important element of agreement between us. We agree that concern for sentient beings such as animals is more important than concern for a human embryo. In contrast, for most Christians who have discussed this issue, the embryo, precisely because it is human, is more important than the life of any nonhuman animal. Most Christians who campaigned against the use of embryos to obtain stem cells did not object to killing animals in research, or even to research that caused suffering to animals. So I think it is important to recognize our agreement here on the idea that sentient life takes precedence and that ethically the most important thing to do is to avoid inflicting suffering on sentient beings.

CHAO-HWEI: Yes, we agree on that. We agree on not inflicting suffering on sentient life. We differ, though, on whether we should respect the strong survival instinct that even a nonconscious being may have. I believe that even nonconscious beings have a strong desire to maintain their survival instinct and that we should respect this desire and not interfere with it unless necessary.

I would also like to clarify that, even though I disagree with discrimination between species, which means that I disagree with those Christians who think that humans are superior to other species, I do think that the potential of the embryo is significant. A human embryo does have the potential to develop into a more fulfilling or more fulfilled state of existence than any other animal species. When we destroy the embryo, we are taking away all these potential developments.

From the Buddhist perspective, life is a continuous process. If the embryonic stage is interfered with by external forces and is forcibly terminated—that is, if the embryo does not survive—then it still has the opportunity to start another life cycle and will develop again. This means it will immediately seek the place of "the next stop." However, will that next stop still be the chance to be born as a human being? Not necessarily. In contrast to animals, a fully developed embryo that is nourished by parental love has more internal and external resources to develop into a fulfilling and beneficial state. An embryo will turn into an individual with a mature personality, emotional and rational balance, as well as a sense of judgment and the ability to tell right from wrong. They will become a person who is able to help not only themself but also others, rather than becoming an animal, which is entirely dominated by instinct. So from the Buddhist view, to develop into a conscious being who can keep cultivating their awareness is a precious opportunity. For a developing embryo, whether it is born as a human or not will lead it to a very different path of life. I hope this point of view is clear.

SINGER: Can we take a moment to reflect on this idea of life as a continuous process? There is a straightforward scientific sense in which life is a continuous process. Scientists believe that life on this planet began more than three billion years ago, and it is likely that every living thing is a descendent of those earliest life-forms. But you seem to be saying more than this. You say that if an embryo does not survive, then it still has the opportunity to restart from another stage of its life cycle and will develop again. You then add that this means it will immediately seek the place of "the next stop." What is the "it" in these sentences? What is doing the seeking? It can't be the embryo itself, because that is dead. Do you see the embryo as embodying some kind of spirit that survives the physical death of the embryo and seeks to be born in some other form of life?

I am aware that when a high lama, such as the Dalai Lama, dies, a search is made for a boy who might be his reincarnation, and that different boys who are thought to be possible reincarnations are presented with an array of objects to see if they choose the one that belonged to the previous lama. Do you believe something like this? If so, do you think there is adequate scientific evidence for it?

I do not believe anything like this. In my view, when I die, that will be the end of me. People may remember me and perhaps still read my books and engage with my ideas, but I will cease to exist, and I will not have left any spirit or soul to be reincarnated in any other living being. I admit that it is possible I am wrong about this, but I would need to see some clear evidence that I will survive the death of my body, and I am not aware of any such evidence.

Even if I did find evidence that conscious beings like you and me survive death, however, it would be a further step to argue that even a nonconscious being has a spirit that survives death. One might believe that conscious beings can, in some sense, survive death but deny that organisms that have never been conscious can do this. So, again, for this to be a reason for me to oppose the killing of embryos in research, I would need to be given some reasons for believing that embryos have a spirit that will survive their physical destruction.

CHAO-HWEI: Your argument poses a challenging question to the nature of this subject. It is true that up to this point, there is a lack of convincing scientific evidence on the whereabouts of "the previous stop" and "the next stop" of humankind. Since ancient times, people talked about their past-life memories with utter confidence. We have more than enough statements from their personal experiences. Interestingly enough, interviews and videos of past-life stories are available on YouTube. Nevertheless, not everyone has that "clairvoyance," and a conclusion based on empirical evidence can never become a universal statement. Therefore, even if these experiences are proven true without exaggeration, and these people are sane (the accuracy of their alleged past-life memories being verified with details such as names and events in relative locations), we should treat such statements with caution. Rather than reaching a straightforward conclusion of "all lives have previous incarnations," we have to consider carefully that based on the aforementioned scientific evidence, we may merely suggest that their lives are indeed extensions of previous lives.

Scientific evidence is neither comprehensive nor convincing enough to prove previous lives. This limitation, however, does not apply only to the subject of previous lives. All evidence is limited to our perspectives and observational tools. As a result, whether the subject is the vastness of the universe or the nature of a microscopic particle, scientific evidence is unable to sustain a universal statement. Over the course of time, with different approaches, a broader or narrower content of observation, and the latest tools, we will discover new facts, and those new facts will be the scientific evidence to disprove previous conclusions.

Please allow me to explain the Buddhist perspective in response to your doubt that even a being without consciousness can have a soul. First, although this being is an embryo, it is still a combination of physical and mental qualities. Its eyes, ears, mouth, and nose may not yet have fully grown, and therefore it is not capable of perceiving its environment with its sensory faculties. Its consciousness might not be sharp; however, it already possesses a certain degree of mental power. The fact that it keeps itself alive and continues to grow as an embryo while its cell division perpetuates is a result of its mental power driving physical functions. As soon as this mental power comes to a halt, the cell division process will not continue, the embryo will cease growing, and it will become a miscarriage or a stillbirth.

Second, this mental power is not called "soul" in Buddhism. Rather, it is regarded as a mental function at a deeper level. According to the Christian view, we have body, mind, and spirit. Spirit is the third form of existence besides body and mind, and it seems permanent and never ceases to exist. In Buddhism, life is considered a combination of spirit and matter. The existence of spirit or matter is dependent on the gathering and dispersion of causes, and it arises, disappears, or changes in accordance with the fluctuation of causes. This combination of spirit and matter may remain relatively stable while all the changes happen, but it cannot be permanent and will at some point cease to exist.

Nonetheless, I appreciate your respect for the idea of reincarnation, which goes beyond the realm of scientific research. This is much more open-minded than just denying reincarnation because you are not aware of this perspective. According to the idea of reincarnation, lives never disappear but continue to return to this world in different forms, one after another. Until we can verify the truth of reincarnation, we do not have to have total faith in any "authority." When we cultivate a meditative mind and have in-depth awareness and observation, we can verify whether the idea of reincarnation is true on our own.

To return to your question. From the Buddhist perspective,

because of strong self-attachment, after death, a life will immediately look for another place, which is its reincarnation—the next life. Let's put aside possible realms other than the human one. If the life is reborn into the human world, it will seek parents who have a parent-child connection with it. With the help of the combination of the parents' genes, the life will then continue its journey. Therefore, after the embryo is killed, it will certainly seek its next potential destination. However, whether that journey still offers an opportunity to be reborn as a human with the help of a combination of genes, you can never tell. If this embryo had an opportunity to develop into a baby and grow as a beloved child in a loving family but instead was killed to be used for research, it might return as an animal suffering inhumane treatment. Then we say that to kill an embryo is to be involved in a negative karmic spiral.

SINGER: May I come back for a moment to the question of population growth? You said earlier that you are not against family planning. I was pleased to hear this, because our planet is already home to eight billion human beings, and it is estimated that there will be at least nine billion by 2050. Do we really want to encourage people to have more children? Doesn't that only add to the problems of the destruction of wilderness, the overfishing and pollution of the oceans, and the emission of greenhouse gases that are already changing the climate in unpredictable and dangerous ways? I see these facts as relevant to what we are discussing, because it explains why we might not, in the present state of the world, want every potential future human being to become an actual future human being.

CHAO-HWEI: Even if we view this issue from the standpoint of utilitarianism, we cannot evaluate it solely with global population and the numbers of embryos that later grow into babies in mind. Rather, we should have a more comprehensive judgment about the complete structure of global population. In the discussion of various kinds of research about stem cells, scientists who wanted to do this research pointed to the medical goal of eliminating sickness and pain and improving health. If that is the goal, then stem cell research aims to extend the lives of human beings. However, don't you think that if human beings extend their lives excessively, that will increase the burden on environmental, social, and human resources? We do not, though, expect living humans to pass away sooner just so that environmental, social, and human resources can be distributed to energetic babies. If this is the case, then the stem cell research that aims at life extension should not continue, and people will deal with illness, pain, and death and view them as natural processes.

You are assuming that the embryo will grow into a human being who has a negative impact on the planet. Why don't we look at it this way: what if this embryo develops and grows up like Peter Singer, who is extremely wise and advocates for effective altruism? Doesn't this greatly benefit the environment and society?

Realistically, of course, we cannot expect that all embryos will grow into human beings who have a positive influence on the world. The concern for Buddhism is respecting the strong desire of all lives, which is to pursue happiness and avoid suffering, as well as to pursue life and avoid death, and to make it essential for our ethical practice. Furthermore, Buddhists regard the whole process of living and dying as suffering, as dukkha. If you take this further and hope to seek a path for lives to be liberated from suffering (dukkha), rather than having this continuous repetition of the cycle of life and death, it encourages us to effectively and completely free ourselves from this suffering, and that is achieved by ascension to nirvana.

SINGER: That last remark prompts me to ask a further question. I assume that we can make choices that bring fewer lives into existence—by deciding not to have children—or we can make choices that bring more lives into existence by deciding to have a child or even several children. Yet if we accept this seemingly obvious truth and combine it with the Buddhist idea you just mentioned—that all life is suffering—it would seem wrong to have children, because that brings more suffering into existence. So Buddhism appears to face a dilemma: either it denies that our reproductive choices affect the number of lives lived, or it implies that we should not have children. Which is it?

CHAO-HWEI: With gratitude I would like to thank you, Peter, for raising a highly challenging question that points out the dilemma in Buddhism. This question inspires me to probe the issue further.

Indeed, Buddhism emphasizes the suffering of birth as well as the suffering of aging, illness, and death. The suffering in our birth is too distant to be remembered; therefore the suffering of aging, illness, and death seem ever more pressing to all human-kind, especially the suffering of death. Human beings are full of fear and disgust toward death; all kinds of religions serve to provide answers and solace about death. To address death, all religions talk about the ability to stay ageless or immortal as an ultimate goal. The only exception is the Buddha, who stated clearly that with birth comes death. We are born because causes and conditions come together. When these factors cease to exist, we will cease to exist. We should not fancy the state of agelessness or immortality. The only way to avoid experiencing the suffering of death is never to be born again. Never to be born again means never to have to experience the suffering of death, and it also means nirvana.

As a result, according to Buddhism, our focus is not the size of the population. The Buddha put his focus on those who had already been conceived and who were already born—he wanted them to have as good a quality of life as possible, which to a certain extent can relieve their physical and mental suffering. Therefore he said that we should try our best to relieve the suffering and improve the happiness of all living beings, including animals. That was his grand purpose when starting Buddhism. In addition, the Buddha tried his best to help people improve their quality of life through correct views, methods, and skills, which means cultivating their awareness and being fully liberated from the suffering of aging, illness, and death.

Thus, to return to your question, Buddhism appears to face a dilemma: either it denies that our reproductive choices affect the number of lives lived, or it implies that we should not have children. Which is it? My answer is that Buddhism does not focus on the size of the population of living beings, nor does it imply we should not give birth to the next generation. The reason we do not focus on the size of the population has been addressed. As for purely giving birth to our next generation, no ethical controversy is involved. Even if we could influence certain couples not to give birth, as long as lives have not reached the state of nirvana, they will find ways to be born in other families, other species, or on other planets.

SINGER: When you say that lives will find ways to be born in other families, it seems that you are actually saying that we *cannot* change the number of lives that will be lived. Do you think there is a fixed number of lives that will be lived, irrespective of whether couples choose to have more children or fewer children? Similarly, do you consider that developments such as the contraceptive pill or the legalization of abortion have had no effect on the number of lives that will be lived? As you refer to other planets, do you believe that even a nuclear war or some other catastrophe that brought about the extinction of all life on this planet, would not mean that fewer lives would be lived?

CHAO-HWEI: Perhaps my answer to your question was oversimplified and so caused some misunderstanding. Your question was that Buddhism appears to face a dilemma; either it denies that our reproductive choices affect the number of lives lived, or it implies that we should not have children. Which is it? To which my answer was according to Buddhism, our focus is not on the size of the population.

It is certain that our reproductive choices affect the number of lives lived. Due to war, famine, plague, the contraceptive pill, the legalization of abortion, and so on, the number of people on this earth will vary drastically. These are historical facts and an experience based on common sense. When I proposed that Buddhism does not focus on the population of living beings, to be precise, I meant that Buddhism puts the emphasis of life in terms of quality over quantity.

However, it is true to say that quality and quantity are interrelated. For example, if the worldwide population already exceeds the carrying capacity of this earth, this situation will definitely influence the quality of lives. Sometimes wars are started to fight for resources, for example, and the size of the population decreases, and the earth becomes more sustainable. However, this cruel means of life deprivation contrasts with the Buddhist goal of eliminating suffering and achieving happiness for all.

Although quality of life matters, it would be ridiculous to sacrifice a certain number of lives in order to improve the quality of other beings' lives.

The contraceptive pill is truly an effective method of reducing the number of lives. According to Roman Catholic doctrine, the union of men and women is given by God, and therefore the use of any methods of contraception (such as the contraceptive pill, condoms, or an intrauterine device) in sexual intercourse is an act against nature and against the will of God. Consequently, methods of artificial birth control are not allowed. Buddhism, however, does not confine its philosophy to the will of God, nor does it fall into a naturalistic fallacy by saying that something is "against nature" and therefore wrong. In my opinion, adequate and harmless methods of artificial contraception should be free of ethical controversy.

Our discussion of suffering might have deviated from the original topic because you pointed out that if Buddhism believes all life is suffering, it would seem wrong to have children because that brings more suffering into existence. Please allow me to resume our previous discussion. When addressing the suffering of birth, instead of referring to all kinds of physical and mental pain in life, Buddhism specifically refers to the suffering of being born—from conception to birth, babies are confined to the uterus and have to be pushed out through the narrow birth canal, which cause all kinds of discomfort.

Even if, in an abortion, an embryo is removed from the womb and thus becomes free from the suffering of birth, a strong sense of self-cherishing drives it to find another suitable place to enter the process of conception and birth. It means that until one finally becomes an arhat, one will keep going through cycles of deaths and rebirths. Most of the time, the suffering of birth is unavoidable.

To illustrate my point clearly, I added "most of the time" in the preceding sentence. Under most circumstances, there are four kinds of unavoidable pain living beings have to go through—birth, aging, illness, and death. However, besides the definite suffering of death, living beings might not necessarily experience the other three. After all, some beings die prematurely and never experience the stages of aging and illness. Some beings (such as divinities) do not go through conception and can be born in an instant; beings like this do not go through the suffering of birth. Nevertheless, this kind of birth is beyond common human experience. The reason I did not provide details of the suffering of birth was to avoid deviation from our main subject, which will inevitably lead to discussions like how to prove the existence of divinities, how to prove that divinities are immune to the suffering of birth, and so on. Trying to prove these statements is similar to trying to prove that *samsara* (the cycle of lives) exists. These statements are beyond common sense or the experience of humankind and cannot be verified by current scientific research.

SINGER: Against this background, may I ask you about your views on the question of abortion? As I am sure you are aware, this has been a heated and polarizing political issue in the United States for the past fifty years. Feminists and liberals typically argue that a woman has a right to decide what happens to her own body and her reproductive system and so should be allowed to terminate a pregnancy for whatever reasons seem sufficient to her. On the other hand, conservatives, especially those with strong Christian beliefs, regard the embryo and fetus as having a right to life from conception.

You are a feminist and are greatly concerned about the status of women, as we discussed in our dialogue on that topic. So, as a feminist, one might expect you to support a woman's right to an abortion whenever she sees that as best. Yet you have just argued strongly against the use of embryos for research, and you have suggested that this is wrong because it prevents the embryo from realizing its potential. In that respect you appear to be in agreement with opponents of abortion in the United States. I am very curious to learn, therefore, what your view is on this controversial question: should a woman be allowed to terminate a pregnancy whenever she decides that it is best for her?

CHAO-HWEI: I consider this ethical question more challenging than using stem cells from embryos for research because it involves the right to life of a baby and its mother's physical autonomy. Both kinds of rights and appeals cause heated debates among Christians, feminists, and liberals. In Taiwan, I also offered ideas from the Buddhist perspective, as I understand it, for this ethical debate. I participated in public hearings and forums organized by the government during the process of amending regulations regarding this issue.

As a result of my reflection on Buddhism, I cannot totally agree with either side of the debate. In my humble work *Buddhist Normative Ethics*, I have defined the Buddhist concept of the Middle Way with the following words according to the meaning in the context of the scripture in which the Middle Way was presented: "To make the relatively best choice, without selfish thought, among the causes and conditions that we see, hear, sense, and know."[3] According to the Buddha's teachings regarding the Middle Way, instead of making a standard regulation and demanding that all pregnant women follow the same set of rules regardless of their circumstances, we might have to make the best choice for each woman relative to her mental and physical conditions as well as her personal circumstances.

For instance, suppose that a pregnancy is endangering both

the mother and the baby, and the threat can be avoided only if one of the two is not kept alive. As bystanders, it is not our place to ask the mother to sacrifice her own life. No one has the right to ask her to give up her life, not even the person whose sperm caused the pregnancy. After all, there is still a difference between meeting one's basic obligations and acting with great virtue. Though we admire heroic mothers who sacrifice their own lives for their children, this should not be regarded as the only moral standard of right action for all mothers.

In this circumstance, although abortion might cause grief, any woman who makes such a decision should feel support for her choice, not guilt, when confronted by religious dogma. Though the idea of nonkilling is valued highly in Buddhism, in a dilemma that involves normal human beings' desire to live, Buddhism treats their desire with compassion and graciousness. All kinds of rules and regulations for monastic vows are documented in the Vinaya, and nonkilling is one of them. However, if a monk or nun's life is at stake and they have to break vows in order to survive, this violation of vows will be dealt with leniently. If under some circumstance, an abortion has to happen, it will cause the karma of killing a life. However, in this context, the karma will be less intense compared with the normal karma of killing.

If this is true of an abortion undertaken to save the life of the pregnant woman, what about an abortion because prenatal testing shows that the baby has serious genetic defects or a rare disease? This is a subject that I discuss with a heavy heart. It seems that whether a child will be able to enjoy happiness and health in their life is a question on a different level from whether they will have the opportunity to live.

In fact, many children with serious illnesses or physical challenges are well taken care of with compassion and therefore experience a strong sense of well-being. Conversely, even if prenatal testing finds no genetic defect or rare disease, that does not guarantee the health and happiness of the child. Over the course of pregnancy, labor, and child growth, many variables can damage the child's health.

This discussion also involves the ethical controversy of eugenics. Are human beings entitled to eliminate the so-called inferior kinds? If this question is answered in the affirmative, then according to the ideals of eugenics, what will happen will not be limited to birth control but will lead to genocides or massacres of physically challenged individuals.

I have expressed a more careful and critical attitude to using embryos for research, even when the embryos cannot yet feel pain. You may wonder why I have a more flexible attitude to the issue of the life or death of a fetus, even when the fetus has already developed the capacity to feel pain. The key difference is, in my view, that both the mother and the baby will directly experience the consequence of the mother's choice. Scientists, on the other hand, have no relationship with the embryos they use. When confronted with a danger to one's personal survival, one might not be able to make the choice with perfect ethical consideration. This circumstance deserves sympathy and graciousness—other people have no right to judge the woman in that situation. Scientists, on the other hand, relate to this issue from a different role. They might have glorified excuses such as saving lives for humankind, but what has often happened is that they justify harm to others with this excuse. The lives being harmed in laboratory experiments include animals, embryos, and adult humans. As a result, I feel it is necessary to draw clear boundaries for scientists and to subject them to pressure so they will seek alternative solutions. Otherwise, their mentality might cause us to slide down an unbearably slippery slope.

Some feminists argue that, because a woman has a right to physical autonomy, we should grant mothers the right of decision-making on abortion in all circumstances. I have some doubts and concerns about this view. After all, it is not easy to prove the concept of "rights" in a philosophical discussion. As soon as the discussion reaches the level of practicality, women in Asia's patriarchal society may still suffer from an oppressive social and relational context. These women include mothers, female embryos, and baby girls. Many women in Asia choose or are forced to abort their child simply because they are carrying a baby girl. So while on the surface the abortion might look like the voluntary choice of the pregnant mother, it is actually an involuntary act under patriarchal oppression. Moreover, this causes social problems like long-term gender imbalance. This phenomenon is particularly serious in China. For babies born between 2001 to 2005, boys outnumber girls at a ratio of 1.1866 to 1, and it became 1.1912 to 1 for babies born during 2006 to 2010. When gender inequality persists, even a baby boy (a healthy one!) would be aborted under the forceful demand of the pregnant woman's husband or boyfriend. Would there really be any embodiment of the pregnant mother's "autonomy"? I remain doubtful.

The reason I became a feminist in the Buddhist community is because I saw how women turned into minorities with physical and mental traumas under the ideas and regulations of gender discrimination. My compassion orients around the minority rather than just women. If, under certain circumstances, women hurt other minorities, I will speak out against their actions. As a result, though I am a feminist, I cannot ignore the plight of babies (especially baby girls) who are treated like minorities under patriarchal ideology.

SINGER: Thank you for this clear statement of your views about abortion under varying circumstances and about the implications of feminism. On the question of feminism and gender discrimination, we are entirely in agreement. Men and women should be equally valued and respected, and there is no justification for preferring to have male children rather than female children. Women have made progress toward equality, and you yourself have contributed to that progress here in Taiwan and in Buddhist thinking. But there is still a long way to go, and women remain in a more subordinate status in some societies than in others. For a man to seek to coerce a woman to terminate her pregnancy against her will is very wrong.

On the other hand, as we already saw earlier in discussing the use of embryos for scientific research, we disagree about whether there is something wrong in ending the life of an embryo that is not yet capable of feeling pain or having any conscious experiences. This is relevant to the issue of abortion, because most abortions—95 percent in the United States—are carried out in the first sixteen weeks of gestation, and I do not think the fetus is conscious at that stage.[4]

You are prepared, with some reluctance, to allow abortion in some circumstances—for example, to save the life of the pregnant woman—in the absence of better alternatives. From the way in which you discuss this question, it seems that only a very weighty reason would be sufficient to justify abortion in your view. In contrast, as I said earlier in our conversation, I do not see anything wrong in ending the life of an embryo or fetus that has never been conscious. You ask me why I do not see something wrong in the loss of the potential human life that could have been lived, but to me, that loss is exactly the same as what happens when a woman decides that she will not become pregnant and bear a child that she would have had except for that decision.

You may say that when a woman decides not to become pregnant, there is no entity that has lost its life. That is true, but if an embryo or fetus has never been conscious, then from the subjective perspective of that being, it has also never existed—or more strictly, it has existed only as a physical object, not as a being with a mental life. This difference leads us to disagree on the question of abortion to avoid having a child who will have a disability or suffer from a disease. Suppose that a couple have decided that they would like to have a child, but when the woman becomes pregnant, they discover the child will have a significant disability—not a lethal one but one that would make the child's life more difficult and would also make it much harder for the parents to meet all the child's needs. Let's also assume, to avoid complication, that at this stage of the pregnancy, the fetus is not yet capable of feeling anything.

I believe that the couple may choose to terminate the pregnancy if, after thought and reflection, that is what they think is best for them and best for their future child. (Note that the expression "their future child" is, at this stage, an open one—it could refer to the child who will develop from the fetus now in the woman's womb if they do not terminate the pregnancy, or if they do terminate the pregnancy, it could refer to a child yet to be conceived.) If the pregnancy is terminated, the potential of this particular fetus will be lost, but the couple will very probably be able to have another child without a disability. So there is no loss of potential, and if the disability is so serious that it is likely to lead to a shorter or more limited life, then the child without the disability may have greater potential than the child with the disability.

Finally, in your discussion of this issue, you touched briefly on eugenics and asked whether human beings are entitled to eliminate the so-called inferior kinds. You said that if we answer this question affirmatively, this will lead to genocides or massacres of physically challenged individuals. Here I have two comments.

First, to allow couples to make their own choices about having, or not having, children with disabilities is not the same as all of us agreeing to label some humans "inferior kinds" and then seeking to eliminate them. It is, rather, recognizing that different couples may have different views about the kind of children they wish to bring up and to whom they are capable of being loving and caring parents, and that we should allow the future parents to make their own decisions in this matter, which will so deeply affect their lives.

Second, we now have several decades of experience, in many different countries, of widely practiced prenatal testing. We know that in the United Kingdom, for example, all pregnant women have a test to see if their fetus has Down syndrome, and when the test is positive, about 90 percent choose to terminate the pregnancy.[5] But this has not led to any genocides or massacres of physically challenged individuals, unless you are going to say that these pregnancy terminations are themselves the genocide or massacre, in which case you are not putting forward any additional reason for not doing what 90 percent of British women think best. Aren't you exaggerating the danger of a slippery slope here?

CHAO-HWEI: I appreciate your response. After our long and thorough discussion, your timely reminder shifts the focus back to the question of the lives of the embryos who are not yet capable of feeling pain or having conscious experiences. In your view, the current state of scientific knowledge does not suggest that early embryos or embryos in the first sixteen weeks of gestation have the capacity to feel pain or have conscious experiences. As a result, you are not against the scientific use of embryos or abortion during this period. Following this logic, if there is convincing evidence to prove that early embryos or embryos in the first sixteen weeks of gestation are indeed capable of feeling pain and having conscious experience, would you have a different opinion?

SINGER: Yes, I would. We would then be in a different situation, with the risk of causing severe pain and suffering to a sentient being. That does not necessarily mean that it would always be wrong to use embryos in research or to have an abortion, but the justification would have to be much stronger, and if the research or abortion were justifiable at all, then all possible steps would need to be taken to avoid inflicting suffering on the embryo.

CHAO-HWEI: According to the Buddhist texts I have studied, an instinctive fear of death is present from the moment a life is conceived. The capacity to feel pain will develop later, and the consciousness necessary to experience anything will gradually grow from obscurity to clarity.

It may now seem to you that there is a difference between a scientific understanding of the world and the Buddhist scriptures, and I am choosing to embrace the latter. In fact, it is likely that in any religious texts, mistakes occurred during the process of hand-copying and passing down through generations. Moreover, any religious literature that includes knowledge of astronomy, geology, biology, and medicine often reflects the understanding of these subjects in the era in which it was written. So I do not accept Buddhist scriptures uncritically. The reason I am inclined to be careful with the previously mentioned ethical controversy is because when there are two opinions based on different views of the facts but no way to find out which one is correct, my ethical judgment will rely on the one that provides more protection for the rights of embryos or babies. After all, once they are deprived of these rights, their opportunities of survival cannot be restored.

Addressing the "loss" from abortion, I believe there is a fundamental difference between the loss of a life that has a potential to live and a woman deciding to put an end to her pregnancy in order to prevent greater loss. The former emphasizes a subject of life deprived of its opportunity to live and the realization of its potential, whereas the latter takes the mother as the subject of life and the embryo as "an outsider" to her life. While she decides to abort the baby, she may or may not feel the loss. On the contrary, she may feel relieved. Even if she does feel a sense of loss, it is a loss of someone outside herself. How can we possibly compare the two losses?

The issue regarding the abortion of a child who will have a disability involves even more complexities. Some babies with severe disabilities, such as conjoined babies who share the same trunk and partial organs, may have the potential to achieve some kind of life. However, in comparison with the endless physical (and quite likely, mental) suffering since their births, the achievement of their potential seems less significant. After all, suffering creates great impact on human lives, and the suffering might not be necessary. It is worth mentioning that the key to the decision to have an abortion lies in the severity of this "disability" and the tolerance parents have toward the specific disability. Some disabilities are not so unbearable to the baby or the person the baby will later become; however, the baby might be aborted simply because of a genetic test result.

You mentioned that the child without the disability may have greater potential than the child with the disability. In my life, I have encountered some individuals with disabilities who, though limited with their physical movements or sensations, have achieved their potential no less than able-bodied people, and some even better. Regarding your example of Down syndrome, I have met children with this genetic disorder. Although their intellect does not meet the average standard, they often demonstrate admirable qualities. Not only do they bring joy to their families, but also their families truly love them for who they are. Therefore, I really hesitate to agree that these children's opportunities to come into this world can be determined sheerly by a test result or decisions that lack thorough consideration.

SINGER: I don't deny that children with Down syndrome have these qualities and that they can bring joy to their families and be loved as much as any other child. Nevertheless, I would leave to the parents the choice of whether to continue the pregnancy that will lead to a child with Down syndrome or to end that pregnancy and, if desired, have another child who will have other qualities. I don't believe that it is up to me, or you, or the state to say that the parents would be wrong to prefer a child without the specific qualities, both positive and negative, that can be expected in a child with Down syndrome.

CHAO-HWEI: Thank you for your comment. I completely agree with you. It is not up to me, you, or the state to decide whether the parents should continue or terminate the pregnancy. As scholars of ethical studies who do not take on any of the consequences of the pregnancy or childbirth, we can offer perspectives on ethical judgment for the parents' reference, but we are not entitled to make the decision for them. If the state apparatus seeks to make the decision for the parents, it could easily fall prey to ideology and political power struggles and be influenced by the desire for economic benefits.

Last but not least, I would like to draw our attention to the ethical controversy of eugenics. You have challenged my point and questioned whether I have exaggerated the danger of a slippery slope. Based on your life experience, you have denied this possibility. It is fair to admit that the chance of a revival of Nazi-like racial hygiene eugenics is slim. However, rather than limiting the scope of our discussion to Europe, I invite you to discuss it at the global level, where there is a great risk of stepping over the fine line between "not allowing children with disabilities to be born" versus "not allowing disabled people to live." Similarly, there are fine lines between "not allowing baby girls to be born" versus "not allowing baby girls to live" and between "allowing parents to decide on abortion" versus "allowing the state to decide." In certain Eastern countries, parents prefer to save resources to raise boys and choose to abort girls. Gender preference like this is similar to what happened in the nineteenth and twentieth centuries, during which several countries promoted eugenics. In order to preserve resources for certain ethnicities with "excellent genes," others were forced to control the number of births.

Some babies are aborted because they will be born with a disability, and some of their disabilities (such as Down syndrome) are so severe that abortion might be a better choice. However, many babies are aborted because their parents only want to support one child or because their country has implemented a strict one-child policy. The reason to insist on having only one child does not involve disability. The second baby might be extremely healthy, even healthier than the first. These circumstances did happen to many families and couples in China from 1979 to 2015. They are classic examples of the slippery slope effects when abortion happened based on the decision couples make for their personal lives and based on consideration of the overall economic prospects of the entire nation.

Under the principle of the Middle Way, I argue that even if we include the consideration of the right to life of a baby or a woman's right to physical autonomy when thinking about abortion, these rights are still insufficient to support a careful decision-making process. Although from a legal perspective, parents (or the pregnant mother alone) have the right to choose abortion or not, from an ethical perspective, parents or the pregnant mother—that is, those whose welfare is most closely related to this decision—should give thorough and thoughtful consideration to the decision based on their seeing, knowing, and awareness in the circumstances in which they find themselves. For example, a child's disability should not be the only standard for abortion. Rather, parents' mental and financial capacity to support this child, the survival instinct of the embryo, and the capacity of the national health care system to help take care of the baby should be taken into account, along with other factors that will vary with the parents' particular circumstances. Only then can the parents make a thoughtful, ethical choice in their individual context.

SINGER: Thank you for this thoughtful response. On the slippery slope question, you are correct that I was thinking primarily of countries with a Western liberal democratic tradition—not only European countries but also the United States, Canada, Australia, and New Zealand. It is true that governments in some other countries have shown themselves to be more willing to coerce their citizens into reproductive decisions that the governments see as being for the greater good of the country as a whole. In this respect, our different views can be traced, not to Buddhism or utilitarianism but to my experiences living in Australia, the United Kingdom, and the United States and your experiences in Taiwan and your familiarity with Asian countries. The danger of a slippery slope needs separate consideration in each country, depending on its cultural and political traditions and its prevailing ideas.

I am also very much in agreement with what you say about the Middle Way, because there you urge that taking an ethical approach to abortion does not mean that we view everything as a choice between the right to life of the embryo and the mother's right to control her own body. Nor does it depend on some objective criteria relating to the extent of the future child's disability. Instead, we should consider the entire set of circumstances in which a couple, or a pregnant woman, are reaching their decision. In doing so, we must be sensitive to the actual consequences that will flow from the decision. To apply some abstract principle or set of rights that are supposed to govern the decision in all possible circumstances would be wrong. We cannot judge whether an act is right and wrong independent of the particular consequences that will flow from it. So although you, Shih Chao-Hwei, and I may differ in our assessment of some of those consequences, when you take what you call the Middle Way, we see another respect in which Buddhist ethics and utilitarian ethics take a broadly similar approach.

CHAPTER 6

Animal Welfare

SINGER: Now, after exploring these different perspectives on taking life, let us turn to something on which I expect we will be more closely in agreement. We first met because we share a commitment to improving animal welfare. How is it that our differing starting points led to the same conclusion?

If I may, I will begin that conversation. I know you are familiar with my book *Animal Liberation*, which you have arranged to have translated in Taiwan, so let me just briefly state the central argument that I put forward there. I start looking at the idea that all humans are equal, a claim that most people believe justifies us in saying that all human beings have rights and entitles all humans to a higher moral status than any nonhuman animal. I point out that although this idea is very widely accepted, once we ask on what human equality is based, we can get into difficulties.

It cannot be that all humans are equal in respect to any particular characteristics, such as height, or weight, or virtue, or rationality, or athletic ability. We should not understand the idea that all humans are equal as a factual claim that describes human beings. Rather, we should say that it is a moral claim about how humans ought to be treated. The best way of understanding this is that we should give equal consideration to the interests of all human beings, regardless of their tribe, race, sex, religion, class, or any of the other characteristics so often used by a dominant group to discriminate against the individuals it oppresses.

Equal consideration means giving equal weight to *similar* interests, so that the same amount of pain, for example, holds the same weight. If after an accident Mei will, unless she gets medical treatment, lose one of her legs, whereas Sue will lose only a toe, then Mei's interest in being treated is much greater than Sue's and should have priority. If, however, Mei and Sue will both suffer the same loss, we should not give preference to either of them on the irrelevant grounds I have mentioned.

All of this is familiar to philosophers who have discussed equality among humans. What is different about my argument in *Animal Liberation* is that I extend it across the species boundary. Equal consideration for all human beings is important, but *all* sentient beings have interests, not only human beings, and if we limit equal consideration to members of our species, we have created another irrelevant category of discrimination: speciesism. As long as a being can feel pain, for example, we should say that similar amounts of pain are equally bad, whether the pain is experienced by a human being or a nonhuman animal.

Many people, on hearing this argument, are likely to ridicule it, so it is important to emphasize that equal consideration for similar interests does not mean equal treatment for very different kinds of beings. Humans and nonhuman animals have some common interests, such as the interest in avoiding severe pain, but they also have different kinds of interests. The principle does not imply that we should treat humans and nonhumans in the same way or even give equal value to their lives. Nevertheless, it provides the basis for a strong critique of the way we treat animals today, because often we give no consideration at all to their interests, or if we do give them some consideration, it is far less than we give to the similar interests of human beings.

CHAO-HWEI: Thank you for this clear explanation of your argument in *Animal Liberation*. I will add, because not everybody has read the book, that you also refute the argument that human beings have a special moral status because of a divine nature within them—for example, that they alone are made in the image of God or that they alone have immortal souls.

The basic principle of Buddhist doctrine is that the operation of causes and conditions come from interdependent origination, because all the factors come together and run together. So based on this principle and our actual experiences, we need to understand that if there are differences between beings, then it is not really easy to say what equality is. Equivalence and equality are rather different things. We do not deny that there are differences between beings—for example, different degrees of goodness, happiness, value, or capacity to feel pain—but we cannot use these differences as a justification for inequality or unequal treatment on the basis of gender, species, or race. I would draw from one of the three important points from Buddhist discourses about equality: like human beings, animals can also experience happiness and suffering and have the strong instinct to avoid suffering and achieve happiness.

First, though, it is important to note that here we can look at the perception of suffering and happiness from two sides. On the one hand, there is the moral patient, the receiver of the actions, such as the sentient being that feels pain, and on the other hand, we have the moral agent. The more awareness, or the more capacity for awareness, this moral agent develops and cultivates, the more this agent can feel empathy with or feel the impact of the suffering inflicted on the moral patient. When we talk about equality from the viewpoint of the moral agent, we are actually talking about how this moral agent can give equal weight to the potential suffering that will be inflicted—for example, to feel the suffering that we inflict on different animals such as pigs or insects and then try to eliminate their suffering and increase their happiness. By doing so, we would discover various perception levels of different moral agents—some are extremely capable of being empathetic to others' pain, whereas some are numb.

You will realize that whether we look at it from the perspective of the moral agent or the moral patient, it is easy to prove the differences between different sentient beings, but it is impossible to prove that they are equals. So how do you justify equality based on differences? That doesn't make sense. It is also equally difficult to prove that, despite the differences, these beings are equal. Hence, there is one standard we can use to make these kinds of judgments, the equal capacity to feel: equal sensitivity. This may be the easiest form of equality to prove, because we think that "since I feel pain, you also feel pain." But the process of proving all this is very complicated. I cannot prove whether the degree of suffering or happiness of another being is the same as or different than mine. So I cannot really make sure that the pain insects such as mosquitoes feel will be comparable to that of other creatures.

Now we come back to the moral agent, because even if we don't know a lot about the being that is the object of an action, we can examine the human moral agent. We have to admit that some human beings, such as psychopaths (serial killers), but also many others, for example in wartime when dealing with their enemies, can be numb and apathetic to others' suffering. Under normal circumstances, even serial killers are capable of feeling others' pain. They are conscious of others' pain, but instead of feeling bad, they are apathetic or even excited by other people's suffering. So one criterion is equal sensitivity in the sense of equal capacity to feel the pain of another, based on the moral agent's ability to sympathize and feel the pain of animals. But examining this further, moral agents have different levels of empathetic sensitivity according to the moral patients they meet. There is a difference between how we feel about the pain of pigs and the pain of mosquitoes, for instance. For this reason, the sense of guilt we feel when killing a human being will be stronger than the sense of guilt we feel for killing a pig. And our general understanding of experiences shows that the sense of guilt we'd feel when killing our mother would be much stronger than the sense of guilt we'd feel when killing other fellow human beings. So even among individuals, there are just so many varieties of "equal sensitivity" when looking at the same moral patients, such as tiny insects. There may be some who are more sensitive and capable than others of feeling the pain of other sentient beings. For those who have this sense, their awareness and capacity to feel the suffering and pain of other creatures will be like working with a magnifying glass; they really feel the pain so much more sharply than people in general do. So they will feel the pain of the mosquitoes as strongly as they feel the pain of human beings. When we talk about equal sensitivity, we must still take into account all these different degrees of sensitivity.

SINGER: I'm not quite sure that I understand the point about the sensitivity of the agent, because most people don't feel any sensitivity when they kill a mosquito, do they? Most people I know would not think anything about killing a mosquito.

CHAO-HWEI: Most people do not, but the people I mentioned at the end of what I just said cultivate this capacity to perceive

154 | THE BUDDHIST AND THE ETHICIST

very clearly what other beings are feeling. They have developed this very strong capability to feel the pain of another, even to the extent of feeling the pain of a mosquito. People like this would rather suffer bites from mosquitoes than kill them. So within the human species, there are widely differing degrees of sensitivity.

SINGER: Is there a view as to where we draw the line, where we reach the limit of this sentience or this capacity for pain? Because we agree that the pig and the mouse have this capacity, and I would agree that some other invertebrate animals also have it. I don't know about insects like mosquitoes. We could try to give them the benefit of the doubt. But at some point, it must end, because not all organisms have this capacity.

Plants are alive, but they are not capable of feeling pain. I have no problem cutting lettuce in my garden and eating it, because I do not think that it is capable of feeling pain. As we get to simpler and simpler organisms—maybe it's a mosquito or maybe it's some kind of worm—we have to make a judgment based on the complexity of the creature's anatomy and physiology and on the nature of its behavior. We may ask whether that behavior is sufficiently complex to require consciousness in order to explain it, or if it can instead be explained in a manner more like the way we would explain the motions of a robot or some other kind of machine, or perhaps just a set of chemical reactions. My approach to deciding where this capacity for suffering actually ends would involve trying to obtain this information and then using it as evidence for the answer I give to the question whether it is likely to be able to feel pain.

CHAO-HWEI: In addressing this question, we must distinguish two perspectives: the public domain and personal comprehension. In the public domain, we fight for giving equal weight to the welfare of all animals. We talk about this on the basis of the general understanding of animals that most people have. However, some people achieve enlightenment, which gives them a special kind of sensitivity to the suffering of other beings. Among these holy persons, some concentrate their attention on their own enlightenment and reach the status we call arhat. Others, whom we call bodhisattvas, focus on reducing the suffering and increasing the happiness of all sentient beings. So may I ask you to clarify the question you are asking? When you ask about where we should draw the line, are you asking about what we do in the public domain? Or are you asking about where those who are enlightened, either arhats or bodhisattvas, draw the line? These are two different things.

SINGER: I understand that if we want to advance the cause of animal welfare, we must, in practice, work with the level of understanding of the general public, and I agree with that.

CHAO-HWEI: In the public domain, what we fight for—since everybody should be able to feel the pain that animals can suffer—is that it is not only the welfare of humans that we need to protect but also the welfare of animals.

SINGER: Right. But my question was a little different. You refer to those who are enlightened as being capable of having empathy with a mosquito, but I asked the question, how do we know if these enlightened people are feeling sympathy when there really is nothing to feel sympathy with? To help you to see the problem I am raising, I added that somewhere there must be a line beyond which there is nothing to feel empathy with. If, for example, somebody says, "I can feel empathy with lettuce when you cut it," I think they are just making a mistake.

I would not think of such a person as enlightened, or at least, not in respect to their sensitivity to suffering. They have gone beyond the evidence available to us about which living things are capable of suffering. That's why I was asking whether there is some standard of evidence required to say that this is empathy with something that might really be there, rather than just something that we might imagine to be there.

CHAO-HWEI: Okay, actually the boundaries lie with the individual moral agents because that will affect their standard. This is the personal domain; this is the result of each individual's personal cultivation of their sensitivity. In response to your question, some enlightened people also feel for plants, and there have been different sayings, for example that "We go to the mountains and cut wood in different seasons based on the natural growth and the natural rhythm of the environment." (This is a saying according to Mencius, the second Sage of China after Confucius.) That's why in the public domain, we need to lay out the standard in terms of the capacity for general understanding, and the domain of personal, private cultivation of sensitivity can be developed according to individual capacity. We need to acknowledge these different degrees of capacity. In the private domain, when the sensitivity may be imagined or exaggerated, that is a personal issue, but when it enters the public domain, there is the line above which an animal's capacity for suffering is so obviously present that we ought not to harm the animal. That will draw the public to some more common ground for the advancement of animal welfare.

In addition, in the private domain, even if one claims a heightened sensitivity and maintains that plants, too, can yell in pain, the only thing that will be damaged is one's credibility if this is ever proven untrue. However, when we are trying to include equal treatment for all beings in the public domain, the general society should be able to understand this boundary and put it into practice. This will draw the public to some more common ground for the advancement of animal welfare. If the general public is required to cultivate its sensitivity to the extent of empathizing with the pain of tiny organisms or plants, it will just make people more confused so they do not know what to do.

SINGER: Yes. I think we are in agreement about the public issue. I'm still puzzled about the other, more personal or private domain. Regarding that private domain, I still want to know, are there right and wrong answers? Or is it entirely subjective?

CHAO-HWEI: You're asking about whether there is a correct view or incorrect view in the private domain?

SINGER: That's right. For example, you said there are some enlightened ones who do sympathize with plants, and I want to know whether that means that I should sympathize with plants too. In the private domain, is there a correct answer to that question? If so, how might I find out what it is? Or would you instead say that some people will sympathize with plants and some won't, and neither view is mistaken.

CHAO-HWEI: In response to your first question about whether there is a right answer and a wrong answer, we cannot verify whether any answer is right or wrong. That is because we cannot know the person's private experience. Also, we do not have a duty to prove whether it is right or wrong, because an answer may be right but be impossible to practice. To illustrate, suppose we agree that we feel the pain of plants and do not want to hurt plants, can we practice it without eating anything? If we don't eat plants, then we starve to death. We have to ask, with these personal sensitivities of arhats and bodhisattvas, whether they are workable or practicable.

In general, Buddhists do not try to prove anything outside the field of experience, because since we cannot share the awareness of others, these things are beyond our capacity to prove. The one area we can work on is finding common ground for our understanding and practice. That is why we focus on this area.

SINGER: I see. So we focus on what we all can understand and what is not dependent on the extended sensitivities of the enlightened ones. Is that right? We focus on the . . .

CHAO-HWEI: The public domain.

SINGER: Right.

CHAO-HWEI: I would like to hear your answer to your own question. How would you draw the line?

SINGER: My view is that we should use our knowledge of the nature of the being. If, for example, we ask whether fish feel pain, a question that has been discussed in some books and articles recently, there are different things we can use as evidence. Because we generally accept that mammals are capable of feeling pain, we may start by asking, in what ways do the brains of fish differ from those of mammals, and in what ways are their brains similar? We can also look at the behavior of fish. We can see how they respond to stimuli that would be painful to us. We have evidence both from the anatomy and physiology of fish and from their behavior. In my view, the evidence shows clearly that fish can feel pain.[1] If, however, we move to the mosquito, I think it's much less clear. The nervous systems of insects are completely different from those of mammals, and the behavior of insects tends to be less flexible, as if it has been preprogrammed. Admittedly, I am generalizing here. Both fish and insects come in many different species, and it is possible that some insects are capable of suffering, but the evidence leaves more room for doubt with insects than it does with fish.

CHAO-HWEI: We also need to consider the observer's capacity for observation. For example, we feel surprised by Rene Descartes's observation that animals are just like machines without the capacity for pain or pleasure. The more aware we are, not only about the observation of the anatomy or behavior but also about the observation of the moral agent, the more aware we are of all these matters and experiences, then the better we can know where we can draw the line for making a judgment.

SINGER: Do we agree, then, that we can draw on the scientific method to reach conclusions on the . . .

CHAO-HWEI: Actually, we need to be aware of the fact that science has been developing, so along with that development, our capacity to become aware of all the other aspects of moral patients can be enhanced. Take the development of the microscope. With the naked eye, we can see many things, but with a microscope we can see more clearly; with additional advanced technology, we can be even more observant. So we need to be even more aware of all these possibilities for enlarging the range of things that we can observe. Let's say that one day in the future it is scientifically proven that mosquitoes, or other insects like ants, feel pain. What can we do?

SINGER: Well, there may still be some things that we can do. We may find, for instance, that the sprays we use against insects cause them to die slowly and painfully, but we could use a different spray that would cause them to die instantly. Even if we cannot live without harming mosquitoes, I would still, as a utilitarian, want to minimize their pain.

CHAO-HWEI: In this aspect we are very, very similar, especially since in Buddhism we are concerned with reducing pain. Even before the time we could scientifically prove that these creatures could feel pain, Confucianism and Buddhism promoted the view that we need to sympathize with other sentient beings because they may feel pain. There is something else, besides scientific evidence. Maybe you are familiar with the debate between Chuang Tzu and another person called Hui Tzu: "How do you know that fish can feel joy?"

SINGER: No, please tell me about it.

CHAO-HWEI: It is from the classic text *Autumn Floods*, in which it is recounted that one day Chuang Tzu and his friend Hui Tzu see a fish, and Chuang Tzu says, "Oh, the fish feels very happy." Hui Tzu says, "How do you know that the fish feels happy?" Chuang Tzu responds, "How do you know that I don't know the fish feels happy?" Then Chuang Tzu's answer is, "I'm standing here, and I see the fish, and I know the fish is happy." What does the story tell us? It raises the problem of our knowledge of other minds.

SINGER: That is a familiar problem in the Western philosophical tradition, of course.

CHAO-HWEI: Yes, certainly. The point that Chuang Tzu is making here is, how do we prove that someone is not capable of feeling others' pain or pleasure? While Hui Tzu suggests that human beings cannot be aware of whether a fish (or other beings) can feel pleasure or not, Chuang Tzu tries to demonstrate that because of this skepticism, Hui Tzu already loses the justification for posing such a question. Chuang Tzu's question was "How do you know that I don't know?" In effect, he was saying, "If you can know that I don't know the fish is happy, then you have the capacity to know the minds of other beings and therefore are capable of winning this philosophical debate. But you cannot prove that I do not know the fish is happy. Therefore, neither of us can know if the fish is happy or not beyond our own personal—and therefore unique—observations."

Here is another way of putting Chuang Tzu's point. It would have been fine if Hui Tzu had just said, "I don't know if the fish is happy. I don't know how you feel. I don't know your observation." But since Hui Tzu tries to challenge Chuang Tzu and asks him how he knows the fish is happy, Hui Tzu must be making some supposition that he knows the mind of Chuang Tzu. If he could prove this supposition, he would at the same time be proving that Chuang Tzu can know the mind of the fish; conversely, if Hui Tzu cannot prove that he can know the mind of Chuang Tzu, how can he prove that Chuang Tzu doesn't know the feelings of the fish? So, to Hui Tzu's question, Chuang Tzu simply answers, "I just know."

When one sympathizes with others, one does not have to prove it, one just knows. Others would not have access to their real feelings and hence can only categorize them as subjective feeling. That is precisely how I would answer your question regarding what I have called the private domain, sensitivity of the moral agent that cannot be turned into public policy. The cultivation of a person's sensitivity is purely personal, and even if their experience is not mistaken, it may not necessarily be transferred into public policy.

Now I would like to talk about issues related to public policy based on Confucianism. In the Confucian literature, there is a story about a dialogue between the Chinese philosopher Mencius and a king. One day the king tells Mencius, "I am not a good king because I'm lustful." Mencius says, "No problem. I am sure you are a good king. One day you saw that one of your subjects was bringing an ox to the court, and you saw that the ox was trembling. So you asked the attendant, 'Where are you going to take this ox?' The attendant responded, 'I'm going to take this ox to be sacrificed so we can use its blood to consecrate the newly cast bell for rituals.' So you replied, 'Please exchange this ox for a sheep, because I cannot bear to see the ox trembling.' The result was that all the people in the country criticized you for being very stingy because you didn't want to kill an ox, but I understand you, because you saw the suffering of the ox and felt sympathetic. However, because you did not see the sheep, it did not occur to you that a sheep also feels pain when being killed."

The conclusion Mencius gives is that all people in power should stay away from kitchens and slaughterhouses. If they are exposed to places where animals are killed, they will become habituated to it, and their sympathy to the suffering of animals will be diminished. And when their sensitivity for the pain of animals is diminished, they will not be good leaders, because they will be less sensitive or not sensitive at all to the suffering of the people. That's the boundary Mencius drew for rulers in the public domain.

SINGER: But you surely don't agree with Mencius's suggestion that political leaders should stay away from the kitchen or slaughterhouse while still eating meat that comes from the slaughterhouse?

CHAO-HWEI: That's why Mencius's conclusion is an interesting one. Mencius cannot deal with the greed or desire that the general public feels for eating meat. Even though the king has the power to ban it, it's not really practical to do so.

SINGER: There's the example of Ashoka in India, isn't there? He was a Buddhist emperor who did try to ban meat eating.

CHAO-HWEI: But it turned out to be impossible.

SINGER: I know. Unfortunately.

CHAO-HWEI: Another emperor in China, Emperor Wu of Liang (Xiao Yan), also tried to ban meat eating because he was a Buddhist. Emperor Wu said that monks should not eat meat, and for the general public, he just set up a rule about certain days on which people should refrain from killing. Thereby he at least made it known to the public that killing animals is an immoral practice. In the public domain, he still took practicality into consideration and only made a policy to reduce the chances of animals being killed instead of banning it altogether.

SINGER: Let's then, move from this to the situation today. If the Buddhist view is that we should treat animals equally in some sense and refrain from causing suffering and killing them unnecessarily, what do you see as the role of Buddhism in the community? Should Buddhists try to educate more people in this direction, to try to promote a vegetarian diet, not just among Buddhist monks or female monastics, but within the lay community? I'm asking the question because this seems to be an implication of Buddhist teachings. In my travels in Buddhist countries, however, I find that almost all the laypeople are eating meat. Is this something that we just have to accept, or can Buddhism do more to oppose eating meat?

CHAO-HWEI: Regarding your question, what is the influence of Buddhism in society? Besides promoting vegetarianism among Buddhist communities, should Buddhists also try to educate more people about being vegetarian? In my opinion, in the past, most Buddhist countries were ruled by a monarchy. Therefore, the monastics actually began to practice the ideal of protecting life within their private domain, rather than protecting animals in the public domain. They became vegetarians, and at the same time, through education, they encouraged others not to harm or kill animals—or better yet, to adopt a vegetarian diet.

In the public domain, both the Buddha and people like Mencius traveled around and tried to persuade rulers to reduce killing, disengage from cruel treatment of citizens, and even provide more merciful treatment for animals. In the Buddha's time, when the Brahmin Uggatasarira tried to sacrifice animals for his ritual, the Buddha successfully dissuaded him. This was the most they could do under the monarchy. In the age of democracy, we must seek to influence not only rulers but also the general public. As a result, we need lobbying, which includes convincing the public, legislators, and officials who are involved with farming, agriculture, and related bureaus. If there is a lack of relevant laws or the existing regulations are not comprehensive, then we try to amend them or initiate new legislation.

SINGER: I completely understand how difficult this is, because I've been working for forty years to get this to happen in Western countries. So I do understand that it's very difficult to persuade people to change their diet. In countries with a Christian tradition, many Christians believe that God gave humankind dominion over animals, which many interpret as meaning we can do whatever we like to animals. And, as you know, the Jewish and Christian traditions teach that humans, but not other animals, are made in the image of God and have immortal souls. All of these beliefs make it easier for people to think that humans are God's special creation and that animals don't really matter.

In countries where people follow Buddhist traditions, one would think that it should be easier to persuade them to stop the practice of eating animals who have been badly treated and then killed in order to make their meat available more cheaply. Buddhist people are brought up with a tradition of compassion for all sentient beings and do not believe that God gave us dominion over the animals or that only humans have immortal souls and are made in the image of God. That's why I was disappointed to discover that the treatment of animals in predominantly Buddhist countries is no better than in Western nations.

CHAO-HWEI: One possible reason for this is that democracy developed much later in Buddhist countries than in Christian countries, so the efforts of Buddhists can be observed more in private cultivation rather than in the public sphere. Apart from personal cultivation, the influence Buddhists try to exercise is to encourage more people to become vegans and vegetarians and to form more alliances to promote vegetarianism. At present, we cannot see more aggressive interference or influence being applied to public policy making.

Let me give you two concrete examples from our work here in Taiwan to explain how Buddhist concepts became public policies and how they have motivated positive personal deeds.

Both examples created powerful influences in Taiwanese society but through different means. First, the Life Conservation Association has always tried to revise and improve animal protection acts. Second, the head of the Tzu Chi Foundation, Master Cheng Yen, has continuously encouraged her followers to adopt a vegetarian diet, which has influenced the majority of the members of this organization, nearly ten million people, to become vegetarians. These are examples of an expansion of positive personal deeds.[2]

SINGER: I am very happy to hear about that, and of course I very much appreciate the delicious vegetarian meals that everyone here is eating at the Kao-Feng Meditation Retreat. Perhaps here in Taiwan, Buddhists have made more progress than in other countries. Thailand, for instance, is a Buddhist country, but there seem to be very few vegetarians there.

CHAO-HWEI: Countries like Thailand, Myanmar, and Sri Lanka, never really did reach the point that occurred in China, such as the time when Emperor Wu of Liang ruled that all the monastic members should refrain from drinking alcohol and eating meat. That didn't happen in countries like Thailand, Sri Lanka, or Myanmar because the monastic members still followed the ancient tradition of the Buddhist practice where they will bring their bowl, and whatever people give to them, they just eat and drink. It's really a pity.

Mendicancy is a tradition passed down from ancient Indian Buddhism. Monastic members are expected to eat what people offer and so have little control over what they eat. The purpose of this is to prevent monastic members from being attached to certain foods and flavors. Since they have little control over what is offered, there is a great possibility that they will have fish or meat in their begging bowls. In response to this situation, the Buddha made three standard rules called "three pure meats": first, meat must not have been prepared specifically for you. Second, you must not have seen, smelled, or been in any way involved in the slaughter of the animal. And third, you must be sure that the animal was not killed for you. These rules are made to lessen circumstances in which animals are slaughtered. Let's take the Buddha as an example. Apart from mendicancy, he sometimes accepted offerings brought to him. If there was fish or meat in a food offering for the Buddha, that meant obviously it was sacrificed for him, so how would he accept such food?

Some monastic members lived in areas like the Mongolian desert or the Tibetan Plateau, where vegetables weren't available, so due to the geographical differences, they adapted to eating meat. However, with improved situations nowadays like the advancement of agriculture and the convenient transportation of produce, there is enough supply of fruits and vegetables even in deserts and cold, high-altitude areas. As for the offerings given mendicants, if the monastic members of the Theravadan Buddhist tradition insisted on a vegetarian diet and refused to eat meat, people would happily and easily provide vegetarian meals for them. Under this circumstance, if it remained difficult for monastic members to become vegetarian, the only explanation would be that they are accustomed to the flavor of meat and find it difficult to change. If the monastic members cannot refrain from eating meat, how can they expect the laypeople to become vegetarians? If monastic members favor meat, it is futile to expect common people to make changes. If monastic leaders are unable to help their communities practice the vow of nonkilling in the form of vegetarianism, then their actions conflict with the teachings of the Buddha.

SINGER: Good. I'm pleased to hear you say that, because it always struck me like that when I visited those countries, but I'm interested to hear a Buddhist confirm it.

CHAO-HWEI: There is a theory that claims eating meat is not related to the possibility of achieving nirvana. My response to such a statement is, "Excuse me. I did not become a vegetarian because I wanted to achieve nirvana or enlightenment. I just don't have the heart to see animals suffer for me." I would add that if you are not capable of feeling the pain of other creatures being slaughtered, how can you possibly achieve enlightenment or nirvana? I do not think people with this kind of belief can achieve nirvana because a very important basis for achieving that state is selflessness—only when we can totally dissolve the attachment to the self can we escape reincarnation at the time of our death. This would mean the complete cessation of rebirths, or nirvana. The key to dissolving the attachment to self is through self-awareness and respect for others, including being sympathetic to the suffering of other beings. If people are fully aware of the great suffering they cause animals through meat eating but still continue to do so and justify their behavior with "eating meat is not related to achieving nirvana," they are clearly selfish.

It is true that achieving nirvana is their goal. However, are they entitled to do anything they want as long as it is not an obstacle to achieving this goal? If this is so, what is the difference between wanting to achieve nirvana and the desire to have other things? Essentially, they are all forms of "I want this" or "I want that," aren't they? Then this "I" is maximized so the ego can totally ignore the suffering of others, correct? This runs completely counter to the transformation that culminates in nirvana based on the insight of selflessness, which eventually leads to the dissolution of the existence of self.

SINGER: There is one more question I would like to ask before we conclude this dialogue about animals. I have been told that there is a Buddhist practice called "mercy release," which involves buying animals from markets—usually animals who would be killed for food—and releasing them into nature. I understand that this happens on a very large scale, occurring quite frequently in every city in China, and perhaps it is also common in Taiwan. But often the animals are released in very unsuitable circumstances, and they die when they are released, or they damage the natural ecology. Even if this is not the case and the animals survive, buying animals from markets would only encourage the producers to breed more animals, so it would not reduce the suffering of animals overall. May I ask you if what I have been told is true, and if so, what is your opinion of this practice?

CHAO-HWEI: Mercy release was a good custom practiced in ancient Buddhist society, originating from the Buddha's time. Uggatasarira, the Brahmin I mentioned earlier, asked the Buddha, "If I sacrifice a large number of animals to worship deities, will this bring me great merit?" The Buddha candidly told him that this act would not bring him any merit. On the contrary, it would cause him misfortune because he would make many beings suffer. He took the Buddha's words into his mind and contemplated for a while. Later, he released all the animals chained at the altar. Before releasing them, he told them, "I wish all of you happiness and freedom."

This act was based on empathy for all beings and was meant to save animals that were about to be killed due to unfortunate circumstances. In ancient times, agrarian societies were accustomed to living around animals, including raising animals in the fields to feed themselves or to earn income. Therefore, to mercifully release them back to the field would not cause any problems. In modern societies, animals are raised commercially in large numbers with intensive farming methods. They cannot be released anywhere like they were in olden times.

Moreover, the development of mercy release has become malpractice in modern times. Those who practice mercy release hope to accumulate merit through this act, which they believe will prevent themselves and their families from disasters and lead them to happy lives. Consequently, what started as a selfless, altruistic, and pure-intended practice has turned into a crafty calculation.

Mercy release has somehow become a ritual that is highly encouraged by religious organizations as if more merit will be accumulated if more animals are released. Such acts in turn have prompted an industry of mercy release. Merchants catch birds and turtles and sell them to organizations that perform this act of releasing "mercifully." Sometimes freshwater turtles are released into the ocean, which is the opposite of releasing them so they can live. Instead, it becomes releasing them to their death. Some aggressive exotic species are released into inappropriate environments, causing many deaths of native animals.

The industry of mercy release causes all kinds of problems. If this practice did not exist, merchants would not actively catch turtles, birds, fish, shrimp, and so on. The more people practice mercy release, the more animals are caught. Imagine if you went to the shops and told the merchants, "We will have a ritual of mercy release tomorrow. Please prepare one thousand birds and two thousand turtles." Wouldn't they then attempt to catch this number of animals to sell?

To reserve animals to be released totally deviates from the ancient idea of releasing animals by chance. Without prearranged orders, merchants would not prey on animals, whereas when they have orders, animals are in danger. After being caught, they are forced to stay in tiny cages or tanks, waiting for rituals of chanting sutras and mantras to finish before they are released. A lot of them are nearly or already dead by this time. In Taiwan, there was even a specific phenomenon: while animals were being released upstream in a river, merchants waited downstream, ready to catch them again. In the woods, when birdcages are opened, merchants cast huge nets, ready to recycle these birds and sell them again. The combination of religion and the industry of mercy release undermines compassion and fosters greed, ignorance, and crime. Therefore, Taiwanese society in general has harshly criticized these religious acts and has prompted our government to make regulations and laws to ban inappropriate mercy release.

It is not fair to say that everyone who practices mercy release has a selfish motivation. There are still many people who practice the act with empathy. Meanwhile, many people in our society turn a blind eye to the cruelty that animals undergo, but some people's conscience hurts, so they perform mercy release to compensate for the suffering they see.

Once, a man secretly released cobras bought at a wet market into a rural area in Taiwan and caused panic among the locals. I condemn dangerous behavior like this, and at the same time, I would like to persuade the public to give up the consumption of snakes. When I was young, I passed by a snake meat shop. Snakes were hung alive right in front of the shop, and their skins were peeled by the shop owner. This cruel image haunts me. As a result, I believe that those who release snakes might be stimulated by these kinds of merciless actions and try to save these beings without thinking about the consequences. We consider our society civilized. If so, why can't we reflect on this matter and condemn and restrain this kind of violence—in this case, against snakes—and blame not only those who release them but also those who consume them?

In Taiwan, I often tell religious organizations and common people who perform mercy release to maintain their compassion and empathy toward all beings but find alternative methods to support merciful acts. For example, only a certain number of animals might benefit from mercy release no matter how often one performs this act. Therefore, it would be more helpful for people to get involved with animal protection through volunteering with an organization or making a donation. When these organizations are funded, they can create more social impact through advocating for animal welfare, making and/or amending laws and regulations regarding animal protection, and even influencing government policies regarding animals to reduce their suffering and increase their welfare. Furthermore, when people want pets, instead of purchasing them at shops, they may consider adopting stray cats and dogs. The stray animals will undergo mercy killing if kept in shelters over a certain time limit. Don't these actions fit the scope of mercy release?

SINGER: There are, unfortunately, many examples of religious practices that were well-intentioned when they began and had good consequences, but when circumstances changed, they failed to adapt. So today, instead of having good consequences, they have very bad ones. In this case, as you point out, not only are the consequences now bad, but the motivation has also changed, and the act of mercy release is pursued for reasons of self-interest.

It is hard for me to understand how anyone could apply the word *mercy* to paying people to capture animals so they can then be released. If one is aware that the animals will be recaptured to be released again, that is even more shocking. Surely it is obvious to everyone that capturing wild animals causes them great stress and suffering.

I hope that your words and perhaps those of other Buddhist leaders—and Taoists too, because I understand that Taoists also practice mercy release—will help to put an end to this cruel practice and instead lead people to support animal protection work that reduces the suffering of animals and so is truly merciful. Thank you for this most interesting discussion.

CHAPTER 7

Euthanasia and Suicide

SINGER: Perhaps this is a good moment to introduce the topic of voluntary euthanasia, because that will shed some light on our views about the issue of how we balance our wish to avoid unnecessary suffering against the view that it is wrong to end life.

CHAO-HWEI: Please do. Would you like to start on that topic?

SINGER: Let me begin by posing a question: can it be rational to end your life? To make this more concrete, I will tell you about Kerry Robertson, who lived in Victoria, the Australian state in which I was born and have spent most of my life. In 2010, when Kerry was fifty-two years old, she was diagnosed with breast cancer. Over the subsequent years, despite treatment, the cancer spread to her bones, lungs, brain, and liver. By March 2019, Kerry decided that the side effects of the treatment she was having were ruining whatever quality of life she had left. She was encouraged, however, by the fact that the parliament of Victoria had passed the Voluntary Assisted Dying Act. Under that legislation, Victorians whose doctors certify that they have less than six months to live and meet other strict conditions can request and receive assistance in dying from their physician.

Kerry discussed her desire to use the legislation with her adult daughters, who both supported her decision. She also talked to her doctor, who agreed to prescribe her a drug that, if she took it, would cause her to fall into a sleep from which she would not wake. It took Kerry and her doctor twenty-six days to go through all the steps prescribed by the new law. After that, a pharmacist delivered the drug the doctor had prescribed. With her daughters by her side, and her favorite music playing, Kerry said goodbye and took the drug. Her daughters later described their mother's death as "beautiful and peaceful."[1] I believe that Kerry Robertson made a rational decision, and I support the law that enabled her to end her life in a dignified manner and without more suffering than she wished to endure.

CHAO-HWEI: I would like to begin my contribution to this discussion by telling you two stories about my own experiences of euthanasia for dogs, not humans. They might seem irrelevant to the topic you have raised, but I will try to show you why they are relevant.

At Buddhist Hong-Shi College, which I cofounded with Venerable Shing-Kuang, there was a stray dog. We adopted him and called him Lucky. Before that, he was caught twice and was nearly euthanized. Fortunately the public shelter that caught him had him scanned and found a microchip showing he belonged to a Life Conservation Association volunteer. The public shelter informed LCA, and bhikkhunis at Hong-Shi Buddhist College adopted him because he couldn't stay in the LCA office.

One day Lucky accidentally ate some poison bait that he found while roaming around. He dragged his body back to the college, evidently in extreme pain, and the chief administrator bhikkhuni at the college immediately took Lucky to the hospital. But the antidote for this poison bait was available only in university hospitals, such as the one at Taiwan University, and only for human beings. There was nothing else that could help him. So the doctor recommended euthanasia. Our chief administrator bhikkhuni called to ask my opinion. I said they should give Lucky euthanasia. I believed that the longer the dying process was, the more he would suffer. Knowing that Lucky would eventually die from the poison, I would rather he suffered less.

In his teachings, the Buddha said that killing causes negative karma, and according to the law of karma, nonvirtuous deeds cause suffering. However, the intention behind the act of killing makes a difference. Most killing causes panic, fear, pain, and anguish. On the other hand, if the intention behind killing is to reduce a great level of suffering and it is effective, I do not think serious karma will ensue from this behavior. Nevertheless, if this act of killing does end up resulting in bad karma and suffering, I am willing to take the consequences.

Now I would like to tell you a story regarding another stray dog. Marco was an Akita, a large Japanese breed. His nature made him friendly with humans but aggressive and extremely territorial toward other dogs. If he encountered dogs, he would bite their necks and swing them heavily back and forth. To protect other dogs in and around our college, we had to keep him chained.

Being chained constantly meant he would not have enough exercise, which might lead to weight gain and muscle atrophy. Therefore, his caretaker, the bhikkhuni Shin-Yu, walked him every day. Eventually, due to multiple problems mostly caused by old age, Marco could not stand anymore and could only lay on his side. I noticed his lameness and could not bear to see him chained. In addition, now that he could only run slowly, he would not pose a threat to other dogs, so I let him loose. As soon as he regained his freedom, he walked to the road right outside our Buddhist college and was struck by a car, injuring his spine. From then on, he suffered urinary and bowel incontinence and gradually became paralyzed. Marco was a large, heavy dog, so taking care of him alone was a difficult task. He was simply too big for Shin-Yu to lift him on her own to facilitate his elimination. As a result, Marco often lay in his own feces and urine. Bedsores, up to five centimeters deep, developed on both sides of his torso.

When I heard of Marco's condition, I asked students to work together to bring him to the yard. I bathed him myself and used a hair dryer to dry his fur. All that night, until dawn, I took care of him. Whenever he cried, I held his abdomen so his hind legs could lift up, and he could eliminate without making a mess of himself. After he was done, he would collapse on the ground, and then I would clean up after him. Students knew I was busy, so they took turns caring for him. As he grew weaker, his caretakers had to press his bladder to help with elimination. Every veterinarian suggested euthanasia. Some bhikkhunis and lay practitioners began to question the purpose of Marco living a life of that kind of quality. It was true that had we put him out of his misery, it would have saved all of us time and energy. Nevertheless, he could still bark, eat, eliminate, and his eyes shone with the determination to live. Would we consider euthanasia if Marco were a person? The answer was a clear no. Therefore, we continued to look after him.

As the weather turned colder and rain became frequent, I decided to move Marco indoors for both his and the caretakers' comfort. At first, he stayed in a building hallway, then I accommodated him in a single guest room, which is normally reserved for honorable guests such as yourself and respected elders. It was the only room big enough to fit Marco, a caregiver, and all the equipment he needed at the same time. He was under intensive care, and many bhikkhunis including myself took turns caring for him.

Marco's health continued to deteriorate. In the afternoon on the last day of his life, my bhikkhuni students took him to a veterinary hospital. The veterinarian said Marco would likely pass away that very night, perhaps around midnight. We knew the hospital closed at 9 P.M., so we were faced with a tough choice. If we let his life end naturally, we risked him dying alone in the hospital. If we wished to be around when he passed away so he could hear our chanting and blessing in the final stage of his life, then euthanasia would be a better choice. It could reduce his suffering during the dying process. In addition, with the veterinarian around, he would also have better care. In the end, we chose euthanasia and brought his remains back to the college ourselves. We believed it was better for Marco to die surrounded by loved ones than for him to embark on that last journey alone.

What am I trying to say with these stories? Many, many animals are put to death, "euthanized." Some of them, of course, are executed on the grounds that there are too many of them, or because they are too aggressive, too weak or too old, and so on. This is also called euthanasia, although obviously the motive is not really to give the animal a good death. Let's put those cases aside and consider only the cases in which we are euthanizing animals because they are experiencing too much suffering. Even in these cases, when we implement euthanasia, we still hesitate and feel reluctant, because we do not know the true will of the animals. If we can see that there is no way in which we can relieve an animal's pain, and out of sympathy for this suffering we are trying to decide whether it's better for the animal to have euthanasia, we cannot, in practice, consider if the animal wishes to die.

I accept that human thinking about dying may be more complicated than that of an animal. It's natural for human beings in a state of pain to have a wish or will to die, but we can also observe a different reaction if the patient receives constant care and love. Then we may observe that the patient starts to feel comfortable or at least starts to feel that they will cope with the state of pain and suffering. So you can see here that the human wish to die actually fluctuates, wavers. This may also happen to animals, as I believe it did with Marco.

What I am challenging is the idea that, when it comes to euthanasia, we have two separate principles, one for humans and the other for animals. In my view, if we cannot apply euthanasia to human beings, then we cannot apply it to animals either. If we think we can perform euthanasia on animals, then we should ask why human beings cannot also have euthanasia. You and I, despite our slight differences, both see the issue in a way that is fundamentally different from that of Christians who assert that we may freely take the lives of animals, but only God can take human life. They also say that no human being may take their own life. We do not draw such a sharp distinction between humans and animals.

According to Buddhism, euthanasia is not a highly recommended choice. However, Buddhist teachings are not against measures that can alleviate the suffering of terminally ill patients. For example, if a patient is going through unnecessary torture due to their illness, it is acceptable to withdraw medically futile treatment. From the Buddhist perspective, it is difficult to draw a very clear line between what is an acceptable case in which to provide euthanasia and what is not. Some people can cope with pain more easily than others. Especially when a person is surrounded by loving caretakers, they may be more willing to live with pain just to spend more time with their caretakers.

There are so many possibilities and variables when it comes to the will of a terminal patient. That is why if euthanasia were legal, it would be a very difficult situation to say when we should provide it. We would have to bring in the ethics experts and make a very, very careful decision. The wish to die may come from disappointment with the absence of caring people close to the patient.

If, however, we consider a situation in which none of these other factors apply, and even with the very best of care and loving support we are still sure that we cannot relieve the pain, I don't see any reason why we should not provide euthanasia. In such a situation we cannot make any other appeals to reasons that should keep the person from dying. The Buddhist approach is to consider this with a more sympathetic attitude. We are very cautious when making such decisions. We are also very careful to warn against using the limits on medical resources as a reason for the patient to speed up the process of dying. There are many factors we should consider here, and we need to draw a distinction between suicide and euthanasia.

We think euthanasia is acceptable when the only factor left for consideration is whether, through death, we can relieve the patient's pain. If that is the only choice, then we do not see why we cannot do it. And given the present situation where there have been new developments in hospice care that we can use to reduce the pain of terminally ill patients, maybe we will not have such a strong demand for euthanasia in the future. Maybe people will choose hospice care rather than immediate euthanasia. However, if the hospice cannot stop the pain, then we cannot stop people from choosing euthanasia, because if you continuously give morphine to a patient then it eventually leads to death anyway.

SINGER: Thank you for this account of your view of euthanasia and the very engaging stories you have told. I agree entirely with the decisions you made with the two dogs. I also agree that we should not have separate standards for humans and nonhuman animals. One difference, of course, is that human beings, or at least human beings when they have their normal mental capacities, can tell us whether they want to die and why. I accept that sometimes people who say they want to die might be expressing some other need, like the fact that they feel people are not caring for them enough, or they may feel frightened about what is going to happen to them and whether the process of dying will be painful. Obviously, people who are very ill and in pain should be given the best possible care.

In addition, it is important to know that most jurisdictions that have legalized physician assistance in dying have safeguards to make sure that a request to die is well considered before it is acted on. You can't just say to your doctor, "Today I want to die," and die that same day. As I mentioned, it took Kerry Robertson twenty-six days to go through the procedures required by Victorian law. That is a long time. For someone in great pain or distress, it would be too long. I hope that in such circumstances it would be possible to comply with the procedures in a shorter time.

In most jurisdictions there is a requirement that after you first request assistance in dying, you must wait for a number of days and then repeat your wish to die. Often you must also consult a second senior doctor or be examined to ensure that you are mentally competent. The length of the "cooling-off" period varies, but it is usually around ten days. That ensures that if you repeat the request to die after the required interval, this is not just a momentary whim or the result of one bad day. We need to strike a balance here. We don't want to make euthanasia or assisted dying too easy, so that some people end their lives when they could still have had a reasonable quality of life, and we don't want to make it too difficult, so that many people suffer unnecessarily.

Given that the law requires a persistent request from a mentally competent patient, we should not try to say that we know better than the patient what they "really" want. In these circumstances, mentally competent patients are in the best position to know what they want. We can give advice, but if patients remain firm in their desire to die and they want medical assistance so they can die peacefully, then in my view the law should allow a doctor to provide that assistance.

CHAO-HWEI: You have been speaking just now about the legal aspect, but I was talking about the mental state of those who say they want to die.

SINGER: We cannot know with certainty what the mental state of another person is. It's too paternalistic to say to the patient, "I know that you have repeatedly said, over ten days, that you want to die, but I can't verify that you really, deep down, want to die, so you can't have the assistance you are seeking." I would rather take the opposite view and say to the patient, "Okay, if you say so, repeat it often enough, and doctors agree that your condition will not improve, then it's your life and your responsibility."

CHAO-HWEI: I agree with that, but I wanted to talk about the possible consequences. As I have said, in such circumstances there is a strong tension between the surface will, which the patient expresses, and a deeper will to survive. Even if the pain is constant and unendurable, there is this instinctive response against the rational decision and surface will of the patient.

SINGER: Yes, but when people are terminally or incurably ill, it isn't just that they desire to die. They also have an objective reason for not wanting to continue to live through all the painful or distressing stages of the remainder of their lives. That makes this situation importantly different from other cases in which people may say that they do not want to live, such as when someone has had a broken relationship. Very often, we know, people feel that they will never get over such a breakup, and perhaps, for a time, they don't want to go on living without the person they love. Yet ultimately most of them do get over the loss and go on to have very good lives for many years. That's another reason why I would accept the rational will of the person—which, as I have said, is not just a momentary desire—as taking priority over what you refer to as the survival instinct.

I see this survival instinct as something that has evolved because it conferred an evolutionary advantage on those who have it, making it more likely that they would survive and so be able to reproduce and care for their offspring. But today, with our more accurate medical diagnoses, this instinct is an unreliable guide to what a person really wants or what is in a person's best interests.

CHAO-HWEI: Because in Taiwan we have hospices that will alleviate the suffering of the patient, we are not under such pressure to use euthanasia. In hospice, we avoid prolonging the dying process, so the patient does not have to endure more pain. There is a slight difference between euthanasia and physician-assisted suicide (PAS). The former practice means a physician intentionally ends a patient's life with drugs; the latter is when a physician knowingly provides a patient with drugs or an injection to enable the patient to perform a life-ending act. However, in various countries, one or both of these practices are available for preventing a patient from the torment of serious illness. Other less aggressive measures also serve the purpose of pain relief and are worth consideration. I will mention two:

1. Hospice palliative care is a specialized form of medical care with a focus on providing support for and relief of patients' physical, mental, and spiritual suffering in order to improve their quality of life.

2. The Patient Right to Autonomy Act was formally implemented in January 2019 in Taiwan. People with certain conditions have the right to make an advance medical directive, a written declaration, to address their wishes. For example, in order to have a peaceful end, they can accept or reject life-sustaining treatment, artificial nutrition, hydration, or other medical care measures in part or in full. They must have one of the following five conditions: terminally ill; in an irreversible coma; in a persistent vegetative state; suffering from severe dementia; or in other disease conditions or states of suffering that are unbearable, incurable, and for which no other appropriate treatment options are available given the medical standards at the time of the disease's occurrence as announced by the central competent authority.

Granted, these two measures cannot fully replace euthanasia or physician-assisted suicide, but they serve to relieve pain and/ or support the will of patients to have a peaceful end. With these two options available, perhaps terminally ill patients will not feel as desperate to choose euthanasia or physician-assisted suicide.

Nonetheless, there is a question worth pondering here. Will a patient who refuses to have life-sustaining treatments undergo the pain of starvation, dehydration, or suffocation and potentially suffer painfully during the dying process? For instance, in America, Theresa Marie Schiavo (who was known as Terri by the media and the general public) was in a persistent vegetative state. Her life was sustained for fifteen years solely by artificial nutrition. In 1998, her husband, Michael Schiavo, petitioned the court to remove her feeding tube and hydration. Terri's parents and siblings could not bear to see her terminally starved and dehydrated, so they started a lawsuit against Michael that lasted for seven years. Eventually, on March 30, 2005, a federal court overruled the appeal of Terri's parents. The next day, she passed away in peace at the age of forty-one. This was the thirteenth day of the third time her feeding tube had been removed. In other words, she was slowly starved and dehydrated until her death.

It is not hard to imagine that the implementation of the Patient Autonomy Act will encourage patients to make medical decisions in advance. They might decide against life-sustaining treatment under the aforementioned five specific conditions. However, when these conditions indeed exist—for example, one falls into a coma or enters a vegetative state and is unable to express one's own will at that time—the Advance Care Plan takes precedence, which means they do not have a chance to change their mind. Neither doctors nor families will be able to know the patient's true will in this situation and can only follow the ACP directive. Therefore, these patients will have nutrition and water tubes removed and gradually die from starvation or dehydration, as

Terri Schiavo did. Because this situation may not be ideal, some people have continued to petition for the legalization of euthanasia even after ACP became law in Taiwan—these petitioners do not wish to suffer a prolonged death and considered ACP not enough to support their autonomy.

SINGER: I can understand why there may still be calls for the legalization of voluntary euthanasia, even though you have an excellent system of hospice palliative care and you have the Patient Right to Autonomy Act. In describing the circumstances in which you think euthanasia may, after very careful consideration, be permissible, you have focused on pain that cannot be relieved, and you have pointed out that with good hospice care and modern techniques for controlling pain, it is now relatively rare for patients to experience pain that cannot be relieved without ending their lives.

You are right about this, although sometimes to relieve pain adequately, a doctor resorts to "terminal sedation"—that is, rendering the patient unconscious, so as to eliminate all suffering and then withdrawing any tubes providing food or fluid. As a result, the patient dies without recovering consciousness. In the United States, some doctors practice this, even in states where physician-assisted dying is illegal. They claim it is legal because the intention is to relieve pain, not to end the patient's life. But in my view, if you put a patient into a situation in which death is inevitable—as it is when you render the patient unconscious and do not feed them—then you are just as responsible for that patient's death as you would be if you gave them a lethal injection.

The more important point, however, is that we know— from surveys of patients who have made use of euthanasia or physician-assisted dying in places where that is legal—that many terminally ill people want to end their lives for reasons other than pain. For example, in Oregon, which was the first jurisdiction in the United States to legalize physician-assisted dying, the state government collects information on why people use the Death with Dignity Act. Remember that all of these patients had been informed by their doctors that they likely had no more than six months to live, and note that patients could give more than one reason for wanting to receive a substance they could use to end their lives. Here are the patients' answers for the most recent year, 2021, as published in the Oregon Health Authority's annual report in 2022:[2]

- Loss of autonomy (93%)
- Decreasing ability to participate in activities that made life enjoyable (92%)
- Loss of dignity (68%)
- Burden on family, friends/caregivers (54%)
- Losing control of bodily functions (47%)
- Inadequate pain control or concern about it (27%)

As you can see, only a minority—just a little more than a quarter—mention pain. I wonder what you think of that. Could you also accept reasons other than unrelievable pain for ending one's life?

CHAO-HWEI: Rather than thinking that patients give more weight to the first five reasons, I believe the advances of modern medicine manage and relieve most clinical pain. Thus, "inadequate pain control or concern about it" makes up only 27 percent of the response data. Patients still care about chronic pain and the torture it brings to life compared with the other five reasons.

Moreover, the first five situations can possibly happen to the general public. Physically disabled individuals and criminals incarcerated for life lose autonomy, but euthanasia is not available. Minority communities lose dignity under circumstances of oppression and discrimination; however, the justification to request euthanasia is absent. Elders, often without illness, feel their ability to participate in beloved activities dwindle with time. They may also feel less control of bodily functions. From both subjective and objective viewpoints, elders and disabled individuals may have concerns about burdening others; nonetheless, as long as they do not have insufferable pain, the burden on others response can hardly be a reason to perform euthanasia on them.

Speaking of older people, I wanted to ask you about the stories I have heard of some countries in Europe, perhaps the Netherlands or Belgium, where euthanasia was legalized, and it has been said that more elderly people moved out of the country. Is that true?

SINGER: The Netherlands, Belgium, and Luxembourg have all legalized voluntary euthanasia, but I am not aware of any evidence that this has caused elderly people to leave. It's significant that it has been possible for doctors to practice voluntary euthanasia in the Netherlands since a court decision in 1984—so, for almost forty years. During that period there have been many different governments, some more liberal and some more conservative, including one led by a Roman Catholic prime minister, but none of these governments has tried to prohibit voluntary euthanasia. That is because most people in the Netherlands, including elderly people, support the legislation, so politically it would not be advantageous for any government to try to repeal it.

In fact, a few years after voluntary euthanasia was legalized in the Netherlands, it was also legalized in Belgium. As you know, Belgium has a border with the Netherlands, and most Belgians also speak Dutch and can watch Dutch television or read Dutch newspapers. They could see, better than the people of any other country, what was happening in the Netherlands, and they wanted it too. Then the same thing happened in another neighboring country, Luxembourg. Euthanasia has broad support in all those countries. In Belgium, there is even a new law to allow children to decide if they want euthanasia.

CHAO-HWEI: At what age?

SINGER: There is no age limit, but the child must be able to understand what the request means, and the child's parents must also approve. In addition, this law only applies to children who are experiencing unbearable suffering that cannot be eased and where death will inevitably come soon.

I should also mention that euthanasia, or to be more precise, physician-assisted dying, is now spreading in North America. It has long been legal in the states of Oregon and Washington, and more recently it was legalized in Montana, California, Vermont, Colorado, Hawaii, Maine, New Jersey, and Washington, DC. It is also legal in Canada. As you mentioned earlier, physician-assisted dying is slightly different from euthanasia as it is practiced in the Netherlands, Luxembourg, and Belgium, because in those countries the doctor can give the patient a lethal injection if they request it. In the parts of the United States I mentioned, as well as in Canada, New Zealand, Switzerland, and all the states of Australia, the law allows the doctor to write a prescription for a drug that the patient can take, so the drug will end the patient's life, but the patient has to be able to take the drug themself.

CHAO-HWEI: They cannot be given the drug through a physician's injection?

SINGER: No, although ethically, I don't see much difference between the two. The main difference is that with physician-assisted dying, the patient must be able to swallow the drug. This can mean that some patients—for example, those with cancer of the esophagus who are unable to swallow anything and are being fed through a tube—cannot use the legislation, whereas if voluntary euthanasia is legal, a doctor can give an injection. Moreover, in some cases, the fact that physician-assisted dying is legal but euthanasia is illegal could actually take away a few good days of life. For example, if paralysis is coming on slowly and you live in California and want assistance in dying, you have to end your life while you are still able to move your arms. In the Netherlands, you could stay alive longer without losing the ability to have a doctor help you to die when you want to die.

I would like to come back to a distinction you mentioned earlier between suicide and euthanasia. Can you say a little more about how you would draw that distinction, and why it is important?

CHAO-HWEI: The issue of suicide is more complicated because there are different reasons that lead people to consider suicide, such as a broken relationship, or the suffering that comes from divorce, or too much pressure on a student who tries hard but performs poorly, or perhaps bankruptcy.

Both Buddhist scriptures and the Vinaya share an account of a group of monks who committed suicide. They practiced a meditation method that made them contemplate all the changes that were taking place within their bodies. Since the monks did not really complete this process, they were actually in-between. You might wonder what the state of in-between means. In the very beginning when someone starts to observe using this meditation method, they may not be ready to clearly observe the internal organs; they may only be able to observe sensations on the outer layers of the skin and muscles, such as pain, itchiness, tingling, numbness, and swelling. As the experience of the observation deepens, they should be able to perceive or observe how the cells and internal organs actually operate and even be able to smell them. This is a process of observation and contemplation. If they are able to go beyond this stage of the process and continue the observation, they perceive that the body actually consists of a collection of tiny particles that appear and disappear instantaneously. And if they go through the process fully, they should be able to perceive that they cannot find an "I" that is permanent, independent, certain, and concrete. At this stage, selflessness is no longer a concept but an actual life experience.

According to the sutra, these monks were in the midst of this observation process. They had gathered concrete observations on how their bodies worked and realized that the physical body is not as wonderful as it seems on the surface, but rather foul and filthy. Being repulsed by this discovery, they wished to end their lives. Therefore, they went to Chandala, members of a lower caste who killed animals and disposed of corpses, and asked them to take their lives. Because of their profession, these people were not afraid to help this group of monks. As a result, the *vihara*—the place where monastics lived and meditated—was soon filled with bloody corpses. Repulsed and frightened by this scene, people reported it to the Buddha. The Buddha went to the vihara and reprimanded the remaining monks, warning them that this was something they should not do.

That is why there is a precept in Buddhism warning against suicide. Traditionally, an additional precept was created when something negative had happened, as the intention in creating new precepts was to prevent the recurrence of such a misunderstanding in the future. Because of the monks' collective suicide, the Buddha made formal vows against suicide for monastics. But can we say that the Buddha always forbade people from committing suicide?

We see some different examples in the agamas, a collection of early Buddhist scriptures, in which the Buddha did not disagree with suicide. Those cases were ones in which people had achieved enlightenment. They had attained nirvana, achieved selflessness, and completely eliminated self-attachment. The significance of the elimination of self-attachment in this context is that the way these enlightened ones ended their lives would not lead to continuation into another life.

Therefore, the question we need to examine here is the difference between the suicide of ones who have attained enlightenment and the suicide of common people. From the Buddhist perspective, when we see how a life goes from this one to the next, there is a very important aspect that is "consciousness." The decisive factor lies in the very last consciousness at the time of death, and here consciousness should not be associated with our intellectual thoughts; perhaps it would be better to refer to this as the state of mind before a person dies. If a person who is crossing between life and death is filled with warmth and happiness and is rather certain they are going to enter a blissful state, then it is easier for that person to enter a more positive, brighter, and better place. On the other hand, if the state of mind of the dying person is more closely associated with dark and negative states, then they are more likely to enter a corresponding negative consciousness. Thus, a person who commits suicide is different from a person who dies as a result of euthanasia, because the person who commits suicide could have good physical health but poor mental health.

When we talk about the mental state of someone who wishes to die, there is both the surface mental state and the deeper mental state. Even if on the surface this person tells themself a thousand times that they want to die, there is an underlying subtle psychological process working where they want to remain attached to their current existence. It is similar to a person who is about to drown who, by instinct, catches the lifesaving device. Even if a person wants to die and tries to stop breathing, all their instincts will drive them to continue to breathe. That's why people who commit suicide will usually take extreme and irreversible measures, such as jumping off a building, hanging themselves, or taking poison, so that the body's instinct cannot resist their will to die.

Before the moment of death, you can see the very strong conflict between the body's survival instinct and a strong will to die. At this time, you are observing the conflict between the surface state of consciousness and the deeper mental state; normally the surface state will feel shaken, and you see a lot of negative emotions arising. Because the enlightened ones are already liberated from such attachments, they do not experience such a conflicted state; common people without this liberation from the self cannot really cope with such dramatic conflict. They may easily panic and be overwhelmed by negative emotions at the moment of death and, as a result, lose their opportunities to move toward the state of luminosity and wonder. That is why the Buddha discouraged suicide for common people—to protect them.

Next, the topic of habitual patterns is worth our attention. As we already mentioned, normally there are reasons that lead to suicide—people may have undergone unfortunate events such as failures in marriage, career, study, or other circumstances. However, it is undeniable that some people will not attempt to take their own lives even if they have gone through these struggles. According to Buddhist philosophy, if one attempts to commit suicide due to these kinds of events, often one may have already cultivated a kind of habitual tendency to deal with difficulties by considering suicide (in this or previous lives). It is not encouraged to develop a pattern like this. Once this habit is formed, instead of developing the motivation to deal with problems and take actions to solve them, one attempts to take one's own life when difficulty arises. I think this is another major reason why the Buddha includes suicide in the precept of nonkilling and tries to prevent people from doing it. A beautiful girl once told me that she constantly thought about committing suicide. I asked her why, and she said that she didn't know of any reasons why she should have such thoughts. She showed me self-inflicted cuts on her wrists, and her parents had to watch her continuously to prevent her from committing suicide. We can describe her as suffering from depression, but why did she do that? From a Buddhist perspective, one possible understanding is that she may have developed the habit that when life becomes difficult and she has to face some ordeal, she resorts to escapism or seeking death as a way out. So euthanasia as a means of shortening the suffering process is rather different from suicide, at least in cases like this.

Thank you. This discussion has been so informative. I am happy to have learned so much about the current legislation and implementation of euthanasia and physician-assisted suicide around the world. Shall we take a short break and then move on to another issue?

CHAPTER 8

The Death Penalty and Killing in War

SINGER: We have been discussing situations in which ending the life of another person may be the right thing to do. In the United States, there is an extensive debate about the death penalty. Do Buddhists have a stance on whether it is ever justifiable to execute murderers?

CHAO-HWEI: This is another highly controversial issue. In Taiwan, Catholic churches and human rights organizations are the main voices advocating the abolition of the death penalty. According to Catholic teachings, "God created man in his own image" (Gen. 1:27). Thus, only God can take away lives (Job 1:21).

The Catholic Church has historically fought to abolish the death penalty. In 1998, Pope John Paul II prayed that "worldwide nations can reach a consensus and understand that we must take urgent and adequate action regarding the abolition of capital punishment." Pope Benedict XVI encouraged social leaders from all countries to "do their best to end the death penalty" in November 2011. And as recently as August 2, 2018, Pope Francis declared that "the death penalty is inadmissible because it is an attack on the inviolability and dignity of the person" (this announcement is included in canon 2267 of the Church's catechism).[1]

In the previous version of canon 2267, the Church reserved the death penalty for exceptional circumstances, "only when capital punishment can protect people from being harmed by an aggressor." Looking deeper, it emphasizes that in reality, "the absolute necessity to execute the death penalty is so slim that it almost does not exist." The 2018 version goes further, as seen in Pope Francis's announcement, and asserts, "The Church . . . works with determination for [the death penalty's] abolition worldwide."[2]

As for human rights organizations, they argue that the death penalty is a form of violence performed by the state. From their point of view, the death penalty is cruel since it doesn't deter criminals, and possible judicial misjudgments may lead to people paying for crimes they did not commit. Nevertheless, these arguments normally incite strong opposition from the general public (especially from victims and their families). Therefore, it seems unlikely that the death penalty will be abolished in Taiwan in the near future.

Some Buddhist venerables in Taiwan have proposed that it is fair for a criminal who takes life to have their own life taken, for it accords with the law of karma. However, there are different situations that can lead to a death sentence. In some countries, homosexuality is punishable by death, and in others political opposition is sufficient grounds for execution. Sometimes people are framed by others, which leads to wrongful conviction. To approach an intricate issue like this with concepts like "an eye for an eye" or "one suffers from the negative karma one commits," we may fall into the trap of generalization and show a lack of thorough consideration. Precisely because of the controversial nature of this topic, I will attempt to lay out the Buddhist point of view in a broader framework and approach the issue with seven points for consideration.

First, have empathy for the victims and their families. According to the law of karma, good consequences follow positive acts, and bad consequences follow evil acts. As a result, even if perpetrators whose guilt is beyond dispute escape the punitive sanction of the law, they cannot escape the law of karma, which enmeshes them with their victims. However, the effect of karma tends to happen in subsequent lifetimes rather than immediately. Capital punishment, on the other hand, is obvious retribution in the current life and can ease the pain of the victims. Therefore, it is understandable why victims and their families are inclined to want to see the perpetrators punished. Their point of view is worthy of empathy. So take victims and their families' trauma into careful consideration, and do not rush to abolish the death penalty. In civilized modern countries, a personal crime is dealt with as a public affair through the penal system. There is a complete process for which the criminal justice system is responsible, including interrogating suspects, finding evidence, and making and executing a verdict. If capital punishment is abolished, retribution through the criminal justice system will not be available, and victims and their families will not be able to resolve the matter through private revenge. Furthermore, the process of victim counseling may not be available in Taiwan. Even if it is, it would take a lot of time and work for the survivors and families to come to the point of forgiveness (if they ever did). If none of these measures are made available to appease or support victims and the death penalty were abolished, how could victims and their families resolve their inner struggles?

Second, respect the will of both victims and criminals. If the death penalty is limited to murder, then the primary victim is not alive anymore, but the family of the primary victim may also be considered victims. There are also some cases in which the death penalty is applied even though the crime is not murder. Such a case occurred in Taiwan in 1989. An airline tycoon's son, Chang Kuo Ming, was kidnapped and held for ransom. His kidnappers did not abuse him and treated him with hospitality. The kidnappers fed Chang Kuo Ming vegetarian food to accommodate his lifestyle in addition to treating him with respect. However, after the police caught the kidnappers, the courts sentenced all three men to death. Laws at that time mandated the death penalty to punish kidnappers for ransom. We believed the actions of the kidnappers were not so severe as to deserve the death penalty, so we petitioned for an extraordinary appeal of the case and presidential amnesty, but neither was approved. So there is a precedent in which the perpetrator is sentenced to death while the victim still lives. Before this incident, the only penalty for kidnapping was capital punishment. After this incident and thanks to the efforts of human rights organizations, there are punishment options for kidnapping for ransom other than the death penalty.

If the law of the state does not bring about a resolution to the desire for personal vengeance, it remains simply an issue involving karmic causality. The two parties are intertwined in this negative karmic connection and hurt each other through many incarnations. There is no way out unless both parties are willing to untangle the feud. If they are unwilling to do so, the goodwill of others is not sufficient to stop this entanglement. Even a bodhisattva, the being who is considered most compassionate, can only encourage both the aggressor and the victim to regain peace of mind through forgiveness or to reconsider the law of karma and know that if they continue to bind each other with this negative connection, greater suffering will ensue. Nevertheless, as a third party, a bodhisattva can only try to guide the pair with reason without favoring either party. Otherwise, it will cause the disfavored party to hold a grudge for the rest of their lives.

Third, to resolve killing with killing is counterproductive. Lord Buddha specifically defined nonkilling as one of the five foundational rules of conduct. It's not only active killing that is banned—even if one praises death, honors death, or coaxes others to die, one has already broken the precept of nonkilling. As a result, solving the problem with killing does not stop the problem; it only causes more killing.

Fourth, there is ethical ambivalence about the execution of the death penalty. According to Buddhist philosophy, both victims and perpetrators are encouraged not to resolve problems through killing. Consequently, to involve a third party to execute the death penalty makes it even more unacceptable. It is recommended that Buddhists do not act as the executioners in death penalty cases. However, if Buddhists refuse to execute the death penalty but agree to keep this system, non-Buddhists will then have to be the executioners. To have this ethical thinking means to hold double standards and having an ambivalent attitude toward the matter.

Nevertheless, when the state uses its public power to execute those convicted of evil crimes, it involves third parties in the process—the prosecutor presents the state's evidence, the judge provides the verdict, and the prison executioner carries out the penalty. Even if misjudgment at the trial can be ruled out and the perpetrator is proven to be guilty with solid evidence, having an innocent third party execute the death penalty enmeshes that third party in the karma of killing.

The major absurdity occurs regarding the prison executioners. If they were given better career opportunities, I believe no

202 | THE BUDDHIST AND THE ETHICIST

one would want to take this job. Individuals who have nothing against these criminals have to end their lives because of their job duties—essentially this is a lot more absurd than victims seeking revenge.

Fifth, there are consequences of the "an eye for an eye" mentality. This is a dreadful concept. Standards of the death penalty can vary from country to country, community to community, and even from one individual to another. If the death penalty is executed according to the standard agreed on by a community, country, or group of individuals, the vicious circle of "an eye for eye" will continue. As long as the notion that a certain level of sin should be punished with death is regarded as justified, it will also justify the heinous crimes of murderers and avengers. For example, the Russian government massacred Chechen independence activists. Chechen women whose husbands, children, or close relatives were killed became known as "black widows" because they conducted subway attacks against innocent Russian civilians as revenge for the death of their family members.

The death penalty is often considered to be the most suitable punishment for serial killers or other heinous criminals. Mentally deranged killers like this are not common. However, once society reaches a consensus to take "an eye for an eye" action, the chances of innocent people dying from "black widows," religious extremists (such as the Taliban or any Islamic jihad organization), violent husbands, or political dissidents are greater than people dying from bloodthirsty killers.

Sixth, we need clarification on the concept of the abolition of the death penalty and corresponding measures. The abolition of the death penalty is commonly associated with releasing convicted killers. It is frightening to imagine convicted killers roaming freely on the streets—their freedom endangers the lives of innocent members of the public. To think like that, however, is to confuse the idea of parole with the abolition of the death penalty. Parole should be sanctioned only after thorough investigation and consideration. From the Buddhist point of view, killing and rape are considered habitual evil deeds and therefore take a long time to develop (and to cure). These inclinations die hard and are unlikely to be deterred simply because of positive religious influence or short-term incarceration. They are like addictions, and their correction takes dedicated long-term work, without which there would be relapses after parole. It is not easy to correct bad deeds and addiction, but it is not impossible. However, some addictive behaviors are habitual patterns accumulated over many lifetimes. Rome wasn't built in a day; effective correction takes a lot more patience and time.

I argue that the abolition of the death penalty does not equal parole. Corresponding measures such as life sentences need to be taken for the abolition to be effective. It makes sense that the general public does not want to pay taxes for prison costs. Prison administration may require prisoners to work and earn their own livings, and maybe even have prisoners compensate the victims and their families with their lifelong incomes.

Seventh, a straightforward interpretation of the law of karma is insufficient. Various elements should be taken into consideration on this issue. According to the Buddhist philosophy of reincarnation, the destination of one life is the beginning of the next. In this regard, the death penalty serves more like the futile act of chopping off the head of an arrow. It means that the individual is executed before correction of their evil deeds is made, so they will carry this negative trait to the next life and torture or harm other innocent lives. While the death penalty solves the problem on the surface, the fundamental issue is not addressed. Therefore, I believe evildoers should spend the rest

204 | THE BUDDHIST AND THE ETHICIST

of their lives in compulsory correction, rather than carrying their damaging habits into the future.

In one of his incarnations as a bodhisattva, Lord Buddha was a king, called King Long-lifespan. When another country invaded, he gave up all his lands and power to avoid people suffering in both countries. He gave his throne to the invader and retreated to the forest with his queen and heirs. Nevertheless, the invader still hunted Lord Buddha down and executed him. While he was being executed, he looked around and saw his son, Prince Longevity, watching among the surrounding crowd. He could see the rage and anguish in his son and calmly said to him, "Confronting anger with anger can never stop this vicious circle. However, confronting anger with compassion will stop the negative loop." After the execution, Prince Longevity did everything he could to avenge his father's death, but in the critical moment, right before he succeeded, he remembered his father's words and tucked his sword back in its sheath. The invading king learned from this and regretted his own behavior. He then gave the country back to Prince Longevity.

In conclusion, a negative action causes a negative result. Nonetheless, no one should be the executor of the retribution. In his action and speech, the Buddha made precepts to stop and prevent killing. He never agreed with or honored revenge or the possibility of retribution. Thus, for Buddhists, to approach the agenda of the abolition of the death penalty with the idea of causality is far from enough. The long-term effects of the death penalty and myriad elements involved should be taken into consideration when addressing this issue.

SINGER: Thank you for this clear and thoughtful account of your Buddhist perspective on capital punishment. Most of the seven points for consideration you mention fit very well with my secular utilitarian perspective, although I do not accept the idea of reincarnation nor that there is any sense in which we survive the death of the body.

I entirely agree that we should have empathy for the victims of crimes, and in the case of murder, the family of the murdered person should count as victims. I also agree that it is important that the state punish people who commit serious crimes; otherwise, people are more likely to take the law into their own hands, which can lead to long-running bloody feuds.

You are right, of course, that the question of the abolition of the death penalty is a separate issue from that of how long a sentence people should serve for their crimes. It is also undeniable that even in the best legal system, mistakes can occur and the wrong person may be convicted. If the person convicted has been executed before the error is discovered, that injustice can never be undone. On the other hand, this is also the case, even if to a lesser degree, when the error is discovered only after someone has spent the best years of their life in prison. There is no ironclad guarantee against such injustice.

One point about your comments that does surprise me is the emphasis you give, especially in your first and third reasons, to the idea of retribution, specifically the belief that capital punishment is the most appropriate form of retribution for a crime such as murder. In your opening remark on this topic, you also suggest that in Taiwan proposals for the abolition of the death penalty face such strong opposition from the families of victims that the death penalty is likely to remain in place for the foreseeable future.

I find this surprising because when I was growing up in Australia during the 1960s there was a strong movement for the abolition of the death penalty. It gradually gained broad support and, during the 1970s, achieved its goal in one Australian state after another, until by 1984 the death penalty had been abolished throughout the country. Over the past thirty years, the issue has largely disappeared from public debates. No major political party is campaigning to bring back capital punishment. Nor do I hear the families of murdered people saying that their desire for retribution is unsatisfied because the murderer is sentenced to a long term in prison instead of being executed.

As you have indicated, the desire for retribution, and especially the idea of killing for retribution, is contrary to important Buddhist principles. Yet that idea plays a more significant role in Taiwan than in Australia, a predominantly secular society with a Christian cultural background. What is true of Australia is also true of many other countries with Christian backgrounds—for example, in all of Europe, including Russia, the only country that has not abolished or suspended the death penalty is Belarus, and most Latin American countries have also gotten rid of it. Would you like to comment on this? Do you see it as a failure of Buddhist thinking to influence Taiwan's policy on this question, or is it, as you mentioned, that Buddhists have different interpretations of their tradition on this issue?

CHAO-HWEI: It is true that even in some Buddhist countries such as Thailand and predominantly Christian countries, the death penalty has not been abolished. Reality suggests no link between religious affiliations and sociopolitical attitudes on the justification of the death penalty. When we examine the demography of capital punishment worldwide, we see the majority of countries with Christian values (like Western Europe, Australia, Canada, Central and South Africa, and South America) are less likely to resort to capital punishment. The United States is the major exception. On the other hand, left-wing communist regimes (such as Russia and China), right-wing despotic nations, and countries like Japan and Taiwan where the idea of retributive justice is prevalent execute people even if Christianity or Buddhism dominates these countries. This phenomenon has to do with the person in power or people's disgust and fear of death row inmates. As a result, although their religious beliefs preach not to kill, generally these countries are still in favor of capital punishment and even seek religious support to justify the death penalty.

For instance, Christians in favor of capital punishment often reference Jehovah killing every Egyptian firstborn son in the Bible, and Buddhists in favor of capital punishment highlight the karma of cause and effect. On the other hand, Christians against capital punishment use "the dignity of (God's) creation" and believe "only God can take lives" to justify their opposition to executions. Buddhists advocating to abolish the death penalty assert that tales of karmic retribution are merely matter-of-fact narration given by the Buddha rather than something that gives us permission to make deliberate judgments to exact revenge. The stories in the Buddhist texts are meant to remind us that retribution only creates a downward spiral of hurt and summons the evil of humanity. This is what I meant when I mentioned that Buddhists have different interpretations of their tradition on this issue.

SINGER: Although our positions on the death penalty appear to be close, I sense that there may be a fundamental difference in Buddhist and utilitarian approaches to punishment. In contrast to those who justify punishment in terms of retribution, which looks to the past, utilitarians look to the future consequences of our actions. Thus, for a utilitarian, the most important question to ask about capital punishment is whether it is a more effective deterrent than other options, such as long-term imprisonment. If, for example, there were clear evidence that capital punishment is such an effective deterrent that for every convicted murderer executed, there would be two fewer murders committed than there would have been if convicted murderers were not executed, then I would support the death penalty for murder. In those circumstances, capital punishment would save more lives than it took.

Whether the death penalty is an effective deterrent has been the subject of many studies, but the most one can say at present is that there is no clear evidence in favor of the death penalty having a stronger deterrent effect than a long term of imprisonment.[3] That is why I oppose the death penalty. I would like to move beyond retributive ideas of punishment and to avoid the finality, as well as the brutality, of executing a person. If, however, new and convincing evidence were to emerge, making it clear that bringing back the death penalty would significantly reduce the number of murders committed, I would change my stance and become an advocate of capital punishment. What would your stance be in such circumstances?

CHAO-HWEI: The Buddhist approach of the Middle Way reflects the same principle of utilitarianism that examines whether the consequences are effective. Buddhist teaching holds at its core, "May all beings be free of suffering and gain happiness." However, Buddhism emphasizes the importance of a kind act as a total process of which all elements are of equal importance—its motivation, its means, and its results. Based on this principle, even if new and convincing evidence were to suggest that the return of capital punishment can substantially reduce the future murder rate, I still hope for an alternative such as the death penalty with reprieve. For example, even though the abolition of the death penalty may not have public support, at least the death penalty with reprieve—that is, a period of time before the execution is carried out—is available. Hence, criminals will not face an immediate execution. During this period of reprieve, I propose providing education for their reformation. The court can then rule in accordance with the murderer's behavior during the reformation. If reprieved criminals are proactive in accepting education and reformation, their sentences might be reduced to life imprisonment, while deterring new murders.

SINGER: Chao-Hwei, in our discussion of capital punishment, you touched on another area of killing on which I would like to learn your views. You told us that Lord Buddha, in one of his incarnations as a bodhisattva, was the king of a country that was invaded. To avoid suffering for people in both countries, Buddha retreated to the forest, yielding his country to the invader. That sounds like pacifism, the view that it is always wrong to wage war. Do Buddhists conclude, from the example Buddha set in that situation, that it is better to yield to an invading force—even to an unjust invasion—than to resist, which would presumably mean attempting to kill as many of the invaders as possible? Is killing in war—even a just war—wrong? Is pacifism the most ethical position?

CHAO-HWEI: Here you have raised an unanswerable question. Without a doubt, the concept of nonkilling is core to the Buddha's teaching. He did not encourage wars because killing is inevitable on the battlefields. However, wars are often unavoidable, even in the Buddha's homeland of Kapilavastu. Later in his life, with skillful means, the Buddha prevented the city of Vaishali from being attacked by Magadha, a great empire in East India ruled by King Ajatashatru.

Before discussing the Buddha's approach to pacifism further, allow me to recount the brief history of the warfare that exterminated the Buddha's home country. Kosala was a huge empire in the middle north of India. Around the beginning of the sixth century B.C.E., Pasenadi, the king of Kosala, got lost when he went hunting with his retinue, unaware that he had entered the northern border of Kapilavastu, the capital of the Shakya clan. He stumbled upon a mansion that belonged to a Shakya nobleman, Mahanama. Vasabha Khattiya, a slave woman of Mahanama, found the hungry, thirsty, and exhausted King Pasenadi and took good care of him. The king fell in love with her (unaware of her real identity). Upon his return to Kosala, he proposed to Vasabha Khattiya. As Kapilavastu was a small country, it could not risk offending Kosala. However, it would be highly inappropriate to marry a low-caste slave woman to royalty due to the taboo imposed by the caste system in India. To close this caste gap, Mahanama adopted Vasabha Khattiya and married his "daughter" to King Pasenadi.

Both King Pasenadi and Vasabha Khattiya were devoted disciples of the Buddha. They had a son named Vidudabha. At a young age, Vidudabha paid a visit to his maternal grandpa's house and sat mischievously on the main seat in the hall. Seeing that, people shouted at him, called him "a bastard son," and claimed that he was not entitled to sit there. This shameful discomfiture enraged Prince Vidudabha, and he vowed to take vengeance against the Shakyas. After his enthronement, Vidudabha immediately sought revenge (and set out with a large army for Kapilavastu). Naturally, the Buddha hoped to protect his homeland. But instead of waging a war in the name of justice, he walked to the battlefield and sat under a tree with scanty shade. Vidudabha saw the Buddha, whom his parents revered, and promptly got off the horse to pay respect. He asked the

Buddha why he sat under a tree with scanty shade and suffered from the exposure of the strong sun, to which the Buddha gently replied, "The shade of my kinsmen keeps me cool." Vidudabha understood and returned home with his army.

Three times Vidudabha marched against the Shakyas, and three times he turned back due to the Buddha's influence. Nevertheless, the shameful past kept haunting him. Driven by strong hatred and ill will, Vidudabha eventually invaded and massacred almost all the Shakyas.

With this story, we learn that the Buddha was obviously anti-war. Having compassion for all sentient beings, he did his best to oppose wars with reasonable persuasion and skillful means of influence. The catastrophic war I have described indicates that its violence was rooted in caste discrimination, which originated from Brahmins' teachings. As a living example, the Buddha openly denounced caste discrimination and rejected the caste system in the sangha with the assertion that "people from all four castes are equal." Nonetheless, the caste system had been so ingrained in Indian society that the effects of reasonable persuasion and skillful means of influence were considerably limited. I believe the Buddha had clearly perceived the fundamental absurdity of this war and understood that caste discrimination should be addressed from the roots. Without this understanding, the vicious circle of retribution will simply continue like endless nightmares, even though they are in the name of justice.

So in answer to your question of whether Buddhists conclude, from the example the Buddha set in that situation, that it is better to yield to an invading force than to resist, I would reply that with his understanding of the cruelty of the battlefield, the Buddha tried his best to prevent wars. However, he did not dissuade Vaishali's preparation of gathering more military resources to defend its country against Ajatashatru's ambitious invasion. He understood that to raise military power in moderation may sometimes decrease the chance of warfare and maintain peace among nations while providing safety to civilians.

Furthermore, I believe the Buddha would not disagree if the defense guaranteed fewer casualties. Please note that the Buddha did not try to convince the Shakyas to surrender, but had he realized nondefense could reduce fatalities and attempting to defend themselves would do the opposite, he would probably have suggested surrender. (As previously mentioned, in one of his former incarnations, the Buddha was King Long-lifespan, who gave up his throne in order to avoid a cruel war that took place in his kingdom.) Therefore, avoiding casualties should be the main goal under the belief of pacifism. Any strategy of military force, defense, or negotiation should be based on this premise. With this understanding, it becomes clear that defense or nondefense are simply strategies, not the major principles to follow. The main goal, as emphasized here, should be reducing casualties. The increasing deaths resulting from a war cannot be justified by the goal of achieving justice. The assertion that killing is always wrong in a war would be an oversimplified principle when addressing a complicated subject like warfare.

Hence, in response to your question of whether pacifism is the most ethical position, I believe that pacifism cannot be represented by inaction and indifference to the collateral damage caused by invasions. That would show a lack of empathy. Not only does such apathy make pacifism look like taking an ambiguous stance to war, but it also encourages invaders to wage devastating wars without any concern, which completely deviates from the purpose of pacifism. Pacifism has the opportunity to be the most ethical position. However, it can only be effective when one makes a careful judgment based on the principles of the Middle Way in each and every unique circumstance.

SINGER: Thank you once again for a very clear account of the Buddhist position. It seems that here the Buddhist view and utilitarian view are similar. Neither takes pacifism as grounds for an absolute prohibition on maintaining a defensive force or, if necessary, using it, even to the point of killing invading forces. Instead, both Buddhism and utilitarianism look at what you describe as the purpose of pacifism, that is, to preserve peace whenever possible and minimize casualties on all sides.

It has been a productive day but also a long one. Shall we draw our dialogue to a close at this point?

CHAO-HWEI: Thank you very much. I am very happy that we could have a wonderful dialogue here. Through the brainstorming process, some rare and precious wisdom arose, and I am grateful for that. There is a Buddhist practice that after we enjoy a wisdom exchange, we say, "Good. Good. Good." In Chinese, it's "Shan-tzai. Shan-tzai. Shan-tzai," and in Sanskrit, it's "Sadhu. Sadhu. Sadhu." Then we are delighted to share the joy of discovering truth (joy of dharma) with all other sentient beings. May all beings attain the joys they seek in accordance with their needs and capacities.

EVERYONE [THE TRANSLATOR, VENERABLES, AND SCHOLARS ATTENDING THE DIALOGUES] CHANTS: Sadhu, Sadhu, Sadhu.

Concluding Reflections

CHAO-HWEI: As I reflect on the completion of our dialogue, I am led to a deep appreciation of this seemingly coincidental yet somehow predetermined opportunity.

The reason I describe this encounter with the word *coincidental* is that you are a renowned philosopher in the West, whereas I am a female Buddhist monastic from a small Asian country. The chances of us crossing each other's path would seem extremely small. Never could I imagine not only that our paths would cross but also that we would derive from our meeting an in-depth philosophical dialogue.

I describe this encounter as coincidental and yet seemingly predetermined because we both share the same passion for animal protection and a common belief in altruism. We used our different theoretical systems to expound on this belief. We found considerable common ground in our philosophical views, and that has provided a solid ground for these dialogues.

The Buddha often mentioned the principles of benefiting self and others, as well as eliminating suffering and attaining happiness. In this sense, it seems Buddhism and utilitarianism share similar views. However, I was not sure to what extent these two schools of thought resembled each other. Buddhism emphasizes the importance of a kind act as a total process in which all elements are of equal importance—its motivation, its means, and its results. Results alone cannot be the only standard by which to examine ethical behavior. Following this logic, Buddhism seems to be close to deontology, which uses the Golden Rule as its reference.

From our dialogue, Peter, your explanation inspired me on this topic. You helped me to understand that the Golden Rule has always been included in utilitarianism, not excluded. I benefited immensely from the following elucidation. You said:

> I think that when our sense of justice tells us that something is unjust, we should treat that as a warning sign that says: "Go back and check the utilitarian calculations. Maybe this is one of those cases where you're ignoring the interests of people who can't speak up for themselves."

Therefore, although justice cannot be a standard in the decision-making process, there may be warning signs that call for caution, knowing there may be miscalculations that could cause problems. This was the first time I had heard this perspective from a master of utilitarianism. With this consideration in mind, utilitarianism seems more understandable and acceptable to me.

In addition, you pointed out that the application of utilitarianism should try to take most beings' well-being into consideration; for example, the welfare of the largest majority of people and animals should be prioritized because normally situations are not as simple as involving the interests of only two people.

> If we have only two people involved—let's say, you and me—then I might ask myself, "Would I like that if it were done to me?" If the answer is no, then I should not do it to you. But there are many situations in which there are more than two people involved, often many more.

From our discussion, I realized that the Golden Rule can be applied to all people who would be influenced by a situation. This is how utilitarians regard the Golden Rule. Peter, your discourse helped me to understand the broader aspects that utilitarianism takes into consideration. When we are able to consider all people and sympathize with them, the Golden Rule is actually included in the process. This way of thinking does not lead to the danger of holism, which considers only overall benefit for the vast majority and sacrifices individual welfare.

Last but not least, for the dilemmatic issue in which we save many innocent lives by reluctantly killing one person, I quoted a story of a bodhisattva's previous incarnation from a Buddhist scripture. From this example, I concluded that when there are no other options, it is permissible to sacrifice oneself or an evil-doer's life in order to save more people's lives. However, it is not acceptable to take an innocent life to save others. Nevertheless, Peter, when you expanded the scope of our dialogue and looked at this discussion from the viewpoint of decision-making for public welfare, it helped me to regard these issues through the eyes of organizational or public decision-makers. A person in this position is unable to avoid the dilemma of decisions that will involve sacrificing more or fewer innocent lives in a given circumstance without having other options.

When a crash is unavoidable, a pilot will divert the plane away from populated cities with tall buildings and market-places. They will choose to land near small villages with less population. People may mourn for the villagers who lose their lives in the plane crash, but no one will blame the pilot for taking innocent lives. This is an example of how utilitarian theory contributes to the public domain. I have to admit that, according to the definition of the Middle Way in Buddhism ("To make the relatively best choice, without selfish thought"), this pilot not only makes a decision in accordance with utilitarianism but also utilizes the wisdom of the Middle Way, although I believe it would be a tough choice with so many things to consider.

SINGER: Thank you for your kind words. First, may I say that your description of yourself is too modest. You are a female Buddhist monastic from a small Asian country, but you are also the author of an excellent book, *Buddhist Normative Ethics*, which has been published in English. Perhaps even more important, and certainly relevant to the chances of our meeting, is that in contrast to the common image of how Buddhist monastics spend their lives, you have been engaged in the world in many different areas. You have told us about what you have done to rectify the unjust subordination of female Buddhist monastics to males, and of course you have played a leading role in promoting compassionate attitudes toward animals and in reducing their suffering. It was that last activity that brought us together, for you founded the Life Conservation Association, a Taiwanese animal rights organization that published a traditional Chinese version of my book *Animal Liberation*, and you wrote the foreword to that edition. That led to my first visit to Taiwan in 2002, when we met and discussed the parallels and differences between Western and Eastern thought about the protection of all sentient beings, and to my subsequent visit in 2014, when I first had the idea of an extended dialogue between us.

This has been an extremely rewarding experience for me. I have been writing about, and teaching, the ethical issues we have been discussing for many decades—some of them, for half a century—but it was not until we started talking that I began to understand and appreciate how these issues might be viewed from a Buddhist perspective. This was not an easy task. We come from different cultural backgrounds and speak different languages that express concepts familiar to people who speak those languages but foreign to those who do not. As a result, we have had to search for the right words to express these ideas. You, with the assistance of Shiao-Ching, your collaborator who is familiar with both Chinese and English, have been a marvelous guide to Buddhism.

Two aspects of your understanding of Buddhism have been very important to the success of our dialogues. First, you have shown me that Buddhism can be understood as a coherent view of the world and of how we should live in this world, without recourse to beliefs that cannot be verified—for example, the belief in reincarnation. If that had not been the case, our dialogue would have come to an impasse at quite an early stage; I would have had to say, quite frankly, that I cannot accept the beliefs on which you rely to explain your approach to the ethical issues we are discussing. Second, as I have already mentioned, you are not one who places overriding importance on achieving enlightenment for yourself. You do not isolate yourself from the world in which so much suffering and injustice exist. Instead, you see the need to act in that world and play your role in reducing that suffering and injustice.

It has been a true intellectual pleasure to have these dialogues with you. Although a part of me is sad that this has come to an end, at the same time, I must add that I am happy and excited by the successful completion of our project! (I am not sure if you can share that feeling, or if you may consider it is inappropriate to become attached to a project like this.)

CHAO-HWEI: This book is a result of our joint effort over the past five years. Both Shiao-Ching, who has been my translator and collaborator, and I are equally happy and excited as you are. These emotions are a natural part of the human experience but don't necessarily become an attachment.

This book is the fruition of our insistence on the pursuit of a good cause. We all have made a large investment of time and effort in this project. We have discussed difficult ideas thoroughly and in depth. To complete such a task, an attachment is necessary, and it is a positive attachment.

In Buddhist teachings, "attachment" is a mental state that can actually be beneficial if we apply it with skillful means. The special term for this kind of positive attachment is "mindfulness." Without this kind of positive attachment, or insistence on acting for a good cause and completing what the cause requires us to do, human beings would likely be lazy and simply indulge in all kinds of desires, which triggers the usual kind of attachment that succumbs to desires. Therefore, practitioners aim to use wisdom to let go of "positive attachment" once they have mastered this insistence on the good cause.

Some Buddhist practitioners emphasize that we must let go of our attachment. However, they have, in fact, ignored that there are different stages of such a practice.

SINGER: Then I am happy that we can both share and enjoy this moment.

Notes

1: The Foundations of Ethics

1. R. M. Hare, *Moral Thinking: Its Levels, Method and Point* (Oxford: Oxford University Press, 1981).
2. In the Samyukta Agama, vol. 8, the original text in Pali goes like this: *Phuṭṭho, bhikkhave, vedeti, phuṭṭho ceteti, phuṭṭho sañjānāti.* (Bhikkhus! Sensation derives from touch, so is thinking process, thus thoughts occur.) *Dutiyadvayasuttaṃ*, SN.35.93/(10) This quote presents the procedure of reaction: emotion, willpower, and reason.

2: Key Buddhist Concepts

1. See Katarzyna de Lazari-Radek and Peter Singer, *The Point of View of the Universe: Sidgwick and Contemporary Ethics* (Oxford: Oxford University Press, 2014).
2. Matthieu Ricard, *Altruism: The Power of Compassion to Change Yourself and the World* (New York: Little, Brown, 2015).

3: Women and Equality

1. *Theravada* in Pali means "School of the Elders." Theravadan Buddhist tribes throughout Southeast Asia think they can present the "primitive Buddhism" style better than Mahayana *buddhis* can.
2. Thanissaro Bhikkhu, trans. "To the Kalamas" (Kalama Sutta, AN III.65), n.d., http://theravadacn.com/Sutta/Kalama2.htm. For online Pali, English, and Chinese versions of the Kalama Sutta, please refer to http://nanda.online-dhamma.net/extra/tipitaka/sutta/anguttara/an03/an03.65.contrast-reading.html.

3. The Six Monks (*sad-vargika-bhiksu*) comprised a group of monks from noble families who were contemporaries of the Buddha. They are frequently mentioned as being guilty of various Vinaya offenses and were reprimanded by the Buddha. Additional monastic vows were created due to their misbehavior. Their names were Nanda, Upananda, Udayin, Chanda, Ashvaka, and Punarvasu. Hence, they have become a collective noun that describes monastics who violate precepts. Although they are referred to as the Six Monks, they did not always break their vows as a group; instead, various members of the group committed misdeeds at different times, as in the example provided in the dialogue.

4. *The Discipline in Four Parts,* volume 12 from CBETA, T22, no. 1428, p. 648a17-c29). The stories of the Six Monks frequently appear in Buddhist canons of rules (*Vinaya*). The Vinaya of Dharmaguptaka (one of the eighteen or twenty early Buddhist schools) contains 60 volumes, and the Six Monks' misbehavior was documented in several stories in 46 volumes. The example I gave was just one regarding rules made due to their misdeeds. For more information regarding the Six Monks, please refer to this thesis: Pandita (Burma), "Who Are the Chabbaggiya Monks and Nuns?" *Journal of Buddhist Ethics,* http://blogs.dickinson.edu/buddhistethics/.

5. CBETA Online, https://cbetaonline.dila.edu.tw/zh/T1428_005.

6. Thanissaro Bhikkhu, trans. "Aniyata: Indefinite Rules," *Bhikkhu Paṭimokkha: The Bhikkhus' Code of Discipline,* 2007, www.accesstoinsight.org/tipitaka/vin/sv/bhikkhu-pati.html#ay.

4: Sexuality

1. 1 Corinthians 7:9.
2. Genesis 38:8-10.
3. Anselm Grün and Shih Chao-Hwei. *Was Glaubst Du? Christentum und Buddhismus im Gespräch* (Muensterschwarzach: Vier Türme Verlag, 2013).

5: Embryo Research and Abortion

1. "Ananda-Garbhavakranti-nirdesa" (the chapter of the Buddha's teaching about entering the womb), in *The Jewel Heap Sutra* (Skt. Maharatnakuta Sutra), volume no. 56 from *Taisho Tripitaka,* Book 11. Reference in Chinese at CBETA Online, http://cbetaonline.dila.edu.tw/zh/T11n0310_p0328a04.

2. For a recent discussion, see David Cyranowski, "How Human Embry-onic Stem Cells Sparked a Revolution," *Nature*, March 20, 2018, 428–30.
3. Chao-Hwei Shih, *Buddhist Normative Ethics* (Dharmadatu Publications, 2014): 97 in the Chinese edition; 127 in the English edition.
4. Lilo T. Strauss, Sonya B. Gamble, Wilda Y. Parker, Douglas A. Cook, Suzanne B. Zane, Saeed Hamdan; Centers for Disease Control Pre-vention, "Abortion Surveillance—United States, 2003," *Morbidity and Mortality Weekly Report Surveillance Summaries* 55, no. SS11 (2006): 1–32. On when the fetus becomes capable of feeling pain, see Hugo Lagercrantz and Jean-Pierre Changeux, "The Emergence of Human Consciousness: From Fetal to Neonatal Life," *Pediatric Research* 65 (2009): 255–60.
5. Ariana Eujung Cha, "Babies with Down Syndrome Are Put on Center Stage in the U.S. Abortion Fight," *Washington Post*, March 5, 2018.

6: Animal Welfare

1. See Victoria Braithwaite, *Do Fish Feel Pain?* (New York: Oxford Univer-sity Press, 2010); Jonathan Balcombe, *What a Fish Knows* (New York: Scientific American/Farrar, Straus & Giroux, 2017).
2. According to the data from a 2008 food consumption survey in Taiwan, the country's vegetarian population is around 10 percent (which trans-lates to 2.3 million based on the population of 2008). This 10 percent of the population includes those who are vegan, those who follow ovo-lacto diets, those who eat vegetables that have come in contact with meat, and people who eat vegetarian on certain days of each month or on other special occasions. Only 2 percent are vegan, whereas the majority are vegetarian only at specific times. The data indicate that people who consider themselves vegetarian mostly make the decision due to religious considerations. A transition is presently underway: instead of being veg-etarian for religious reasons, more people are becoming vegetarians for health reasons, which follows the trend of international vegetarianism.

According to the Chinese Television System in 2017, more than 2.5 million Taiwanese are regular vegetarians, which exceeds the 2008 survey's 10 percent of the population. Taiwan is ranked number two worldwide of countries with large numbers of vegetarian restaurants.

These data (in Chinese) are from "The Food Institute Is Optimistic about the Vegetarian Industry and Estimates the Size of the Vegetarian Market in Taiwan at NTD 59 Billion," Suiis Point of View, September

18, 2009, www.suiis.com/view/ViewArticle.asp?no=1014#axzz3ESBh-

jqlr; and "Taiwan's Vegetarian Population Exceeds 10%, Ranking Second in the World," CTS, October 18, 2017, http://news.cts.com.tw/cts
/life/201710/20171018189515s.html#.Wo2dEoNub.

7: Euthanasia and Suicide

1. "Bendigo Woman Kerry Robertson Becomes First Victorian to Use
   Voluntary Assisted Dying Act," ABC News, updated August 5, 2019,
   www.abc.net.au/news/2019-08-04/bendigo-woman-first-victorian
   -use-voluntary-assisted-dying-law/11382332.
2. Oregon Health Authority, Oregon Death with Dignity Act: 2021 Data
   Summary, OHA, February 28, 2022, www.oregon.gov/oha/ph/provider
   partnerresources/evaluationresearch/deathwithdignityact/Pages
   /index.aspx.

8: The Death Penalty and Killing in War

1. Information (in Chinese) about the Catholic Church's official statement
   for the abolition of the death penalty can be found in "The Catholic
   Church Will Push for the Global Abolition of the Death Penalty. Pope
   Francis Declares: The Death Penalty Is Inadmissible under All Circumstances," Storm Media, August 2, 2018, www.storm.mg/article/471733.
2. Ibid.
3. See, for example, Daniel Nagin, "Deterrence and the Death Penalty:
   Why the Statistics Should be Ignored," Royal Statistical Society, May
   2, 2014, https://doi.org/10.1111/j.1740-9713.2014.00733.x.

Index

About the Authors

PETER SINGER was born in Melbourne, Australia, in 1946 and educated at the University of Melbourne and the University of Oxford. Having taught in England, the United States, and Australia, he has been the Ira W. DeCamp Professor of Bioethics in the University Center for Human Values at Princeton University since 1999.

Singer first became well known internationally after the publication of his book *Animal Liberation* in 1975. A fully revised and updated version, *Animal Liberation Now,* was published in 2023. Another of his books, *The Life You Can Save*, first published in 2009, led him to found a nonprofit organization of the same name that has raised more than US$85 million for the most effective charities assisting people in extreme poverty. Singer subsequently made an updated edition of that book available, free, from www.thelifeyoucansave.org. Singer has written, coauthored, edited, or coedited more than fifty books, and his writings have been translated into more than thirty languages. Some of his other well-known publications include *Practical Ethics*, *The Expanding Circle*, *Rethinking Life and Death*, *Ethics in the Real World*, and *Why Vegan?*

In 2012, Singer was made a Companion of the Order of Australia, the nation's highest civic honor. Since 2021, he has been a founding coeditor of the *Journal of Controversial Ideas*, which promotes freedom of thought and discussion, pushing back against restrictions on what can be published. Also in 2021, he was awarded the $1 million Berggruen Prize for Philosophy and Culture, and he divided the prize money between the most effective charities saving and improving the lives of people in extreme poverty and those working to reduce the suffering of animals.

SHIH CHAO-HWEI was born in Yangon, Myanmar, in 1958. Venerable Shih Chao-Hwei's ancestry traces back to Mei County in Kuang-Dong Province, China. She graduated from the Department of Chinese at National Taiwan Normal University. Currently, she teaches in the Religion and Culture Department at Hsuan-Chuang University in Hsin-Chu, Taiwan, and previously served as the head of the department and the dean of the university's Social Science School.

As an animal lover who could not bear to see animals suffer, she founded the Life Conservation Association in 1993 to improve animal welfare in Taiwan. Shih Chao-Hwei took her bhikkhuni vows in 1978 and personally studied with Master Yin Shun for decades, which led her to recognize the importance of proper Buddhist education. As a result, she founded Buddhist Hong-Shi College in Taiwan to offer a space and selection of courses for Buddhist studies and monastic education.

As a prolific Buddhist scholar, Shih Chao-Hwei has published thirty-four books and eighty papers for journals to date. In 2007, the founder of INEB (International Network of Engaged Buddhists based in Thailand), Professor Sulak Sivaraksa invited her to be a spiritual mentor of the organization along with His Holiness the Fourteenth Dalai Lama, Thich Nhat Hanh, and Buddhadasa Bhikkhu. The same year, Shih Chao-Hwei received the Chinese Literary Award for cultural discourse from the Chinese Literature and Arts Association, Taiwan. And in 2021, she received Japan's Niwano Peace Prize, which is known worldwide as the Religious Nobel Prize.